CW01617535

CONTE

SECTION ONE — Thou Shalt Love...

SECTION TWO — ...The Lord thy God

SECTION THREE — Jesus Christ

SECTION FOUR — The Holy Spirit

Day by day
with the love of God

THOU SHALT LOVE..

DOROTHY B. KING

With Foreword by Patience Strong

DENHOLM HOUSE PRESS
Robert Denholm House
Nutfield, Surrey RH1 4HW

First published 1974

ISBN 0 85213 098 8

THIS BOOK IS DEDICATED TO
MY FRIENDS ALL ROUND THE WORLD

Cover Design: Donald Grey

Printed in Hungary by the
Alföldi Printing House, Decrecen

FOREWORD
by Patience Strong

The trouble today with the world in general and with our own country in particular is that there are too few Dorothy Kings around to leaven the lump of materialism with the yeasty spirit of a religion with life in it, a religion that is both mystical and practical, active and contemplative: in short, the gospel as taught by our Lord Himself.

The uncompromising rule of Divine priority runs like a golden thread through this helpful and inspired little book with its emphasis on the necessity of putting God first. If you do indeed love God with all your heart, soul and mind, how can you not love your neighbour? Love is the fulfilling of the law, wrote St. Paul, and he declared love to be greater than faith or hope.

The word love is one of the holy words of life, but like many other sacred things in this unholy age it has become tarnished. It is now a blanket word covering every kind of affection. Failure to understand its true meaning has been partially responsible for bringing about the so-called permissive society, and what mischief that ambiguous term has bred!

What is permitted and by whom? The dreary and deadly consequences of the moral laxity which the term encouraged can be seen all around us in the weakening of family ties, indifference to religion and a lowering of standards in dress and behaviour.

The kind of love that this book is all about is the love that gives and is costly, and it is no respecter of persons, for Christian love demands that we act and speak with charity even to those whom we may dislike. This love is a solvent, melting away all that is hard and unforgiving in human nature. Love one another, said Jesus. Why do we not try it? In Chesterton's often quoted assertion, the Christian ideal has not been tried and found wanting; it has been found difficult; and left untried.

When, about three years ago, I received a letter from Mrs. King asking me if I would speak at a meeting in Weymouth it was impossible for me to undertake outside engagements. But Dorothy King was not the sort of person to take No for an answer. I showed her second letter to my husband who said, "You couldn't disappoint the writer of a letter such as this". I couldn't; so I went.

I expected to see a calm elderly lady. In fact, I was swept off my feet by her gay warm-hearted reception. Here, I thought, is someone who will never grow old; she has within her the secret of perennial youth, for she is in love with everybody, a whirlwind of energy ever busy about the Lord's business, giving out all the time; one who not only preaches but practises the first commandment and who draws her spiritual and physical vitality from a faith that is renewed by prayer in the early hours of every new day.

Her book is a treasure; a book to keep and a book to give.

PATIENCE STRONG

ACKNOWLEDGEMENTS

The author and publishers wish to thank the following for permission to use copyright material. Every effort has been made to trace the source of quotations and if any remain unacknowledged the necessary amendments will be made in subsequent editions.

Associated Book Publishers Ltd, No. 67 (*In the steps of the Master,* H. V. Morton, published Methuen and Co., Ltd).
The Bible Reading Fellowship, Nos. 15, 28, 77, 81, 113, 116.
Cambridge University Press, Nos. 20, 67 (New English Bible, Second Edition, copyright 1970).
Church Pastoral Aid Society, Nos. 85, 88 (Watson, *My God is Real*).
Collins, Nos. 16 (M. v. Trapp, *The Sound of Music*), 17 (Phillips, *N. T. in Modern English*).
Darton, Longman and Todd Ltd. (and Doubleday and Co. Inc.), Nos. 11, 13 (Jerusalem Bible).
Dunamis Charismatic Magazine, No. 114.
Free Church Federal Council, No. 96 (Harris).
Fontana Books (Collins), Nos. 18, 30 (King, *Strength to Love*).
Fountain Trust, Nos. 102, 111, 114 *(Renewal)*.
Friends Home Service Committee, No. 60 (Hodgkin, *Fierce Feathers*).
Inter-Varsity Press, Nos. 103, 119 (Stott).
Hodder and Stoughton Limited, Nos. 12 (Gray), 17, 35, 99 (Weatherhead), 19 (Grayson, *Adventures in Understanding*), 25, 29 (Moffat *New Testament*), 61, 62, 63, 64, 80, 84 (Paterson Smyth, *A People's Life of Christ*), 87 (Solis-Cohen), 89 (Nicoll, *Seen and Unseen*), 112, 113 (Chadwick, *The Path of Prayer*).
Logos, Nos. 100, 101, 102 (Bennett).
Lutterworth Press, 96 (Grubb, *C. T. Studd*).
Methodist Publishing House, Nos, 2, 5, 13, 14, 24, 39, 66, 117, 120 (Sangster). 41 (Blatchford), 78 (*The Promise Book,* I. and L. Church), 91, 94 (Barclay, *The Promise of the Spirit*).
Methodist Recorder, 48 (M. Harwood), 56 (James).
Frederick Muller Ltd., Nos. 8, 17, 31, 49, 56 (P. Strong, *Birthday Book*).
Oxford University Press, 63 (Housman, *The Maker of the Sun and Moon* from the *English Hymnal*).
S. P. C. K, Nos. 4, 8, 16, 23, 32, 57, 108, (Hoyland, *Book of Prayers for use in an Indian College*), 14 (Milner-White, *My God My Glory*).
The Saint Andrew Press, Nos. 75, 80, 86, 97 (Barclay, *The Daily Study Bible*).

The following have also kindly given their permission:

Canon Clifford-Pronger, No. 86. Rev. T. J. Foinette, No. 32. Canon M. Heath Garner, No. 59. The Ernest Luff Homes, No. 4. Mrs Norah Mitchell, No. 86 (hymn by E. L. Budry).

PREFACE

The theme of this book is LOVE. 'Thou shalt love the Lord thy God with all thy heart, and with all thy soul, and with all thy mind, and with all thy strength, and thy neighbour as thyself.' These, Jesus declared, are the Great Commandments.

Our world's survival depends upon our obeying these commandments. Violence and hate destroy. Love builds up. The world needs love—and we can build each other up in love. Even those who act maliciously, Jesus said, must be loved.

The book is suitable for daily use if so desired. It has four sections. The first treats the Commandment itself, 'Thou shalt love...'; the other three deal with the Godhead—God the Father, Jesus Christ the Son, and the Holy Spirit. On each page are passages from the Bible, with comments from many other sources, many of which I have collected and been helped by through the years. Each page closes with a prayer. It is hoped fo publish two further books to cover the text which begins this preface.

The Authorised Version of the Bible has generally been used and most of the hymns quoted appear in the Methodist Hymn Book. Passages not attributed to any source or author may be regarded as from the compiler.

May God use this book, helping each reader to grow daily in His love.

Gratefully I acknowledge the debt I owe to the writers of quotations I have used. I especially want also to thank the Rev. Dr. Frank Cumbers (formerly, for many years, of the Epworth Press) and the Rev. Paul Morton-George of Denholm House Press, for their valuable assistance in preparing this book.

Frinton-on-Sea, Essex 1974 DOROTHY B. KING

SECTION ONE – Thou Shalt Love...

1. In the Beginning

In the beginning, God.... *Gen 1: 1*
God is love. *1 John 4: 8*

Since our theme is love, the beginning must be with God, for God is love. We are all God's children; to each of us He has given part of Himself—the power to love and to be loved. The world's very existence depends on love. God wants us to reflect His love. Each one of us can help to dissipate the world's hatred by obeying His command to love. Love can do the impossible things!
Rev. Harry Bisseker of Leys School, Cambridge, once said that the sun's rays are pure white, but are reflected on the earth by different colours—green grass, red roses ... but all these colours together make up the pure white! So with our love. Some are drawn to God by a Salvation Army girl's love, others through some learned professor, and so on.

Come let us sing of a wonderful love,
  Tender and true;
Out of the heart of the Father above,
  Streaming to me and to you:
    Wonderful Love
Dwells in the heart of the Father above.

ROBERT WALMSLEY

Dear God, who art the Creator of all life, we lift up our hearts to Thee in praise, in thanksgiving and in love, knowing that Thou who art love carest for each one of Thy children, the wide world over. Thou hast given us each one the power to love; it is Thy great gift to us, which can transform our whole being.

2. Thou shalt Love

Hear, O Israel: The Lord our God is one Lord: and thou shalt love the Lord thy God with all thine heart, and with all thy soul, and with all thy might. And these words, which I command thee this day, shall be in thine heart. *Deuteronomy 6: 4–6*

O ye who taste that love is sweet,
Set waymarks for all doubtful feet
That stumble on in search of it.

Sing notes of love; that some who hear
Far off, inert, may lend an ear,
Rise up and wonder and draw near.

Lead lives of love; that others who
Behold your life may kindle too
With love, and cast their lot with you.

CHRISTINA ROSSETTI

Having seen the love of God, his own love leaps in response. His heart is drawn out of him and lost in God's immensity. Passion enslaves us: the love which God gives sets us free. Passion blinds us to the defects of the loved one: this love sees the defects in other mortals, but loves just the same. It is by love that man comes to freedom, and there is no other way.

W. E. SANGSTER

Lord —
How shall I thank Thee for the grace
On me and all mankind bestowed?
O that my every breath were praise!
O that my heart were filled with God!
My heart would then with love o'erflow,
And all my life Thy glory show. CHARLES WESLEY

3. The Law of Love

And now, Israel, what doth the Lord thy God require of thee, but to fear the Lord thy God, to walk in all his ways, and to love him, and to serve the Lord thy God with all thy heart and with all thy soul, to keep the commandments of the Lord, and his statutes, which I command thee this day for thy good.

Deuteronomy 10: 12, 13.

Belovèd, let us love;
  Love is of God;
In God alone hath love
  Its true abode.

Belovèd, let us love:
  For they who love,
They only are His sons,
  Born from above.

Belovèd, let us love:
  In love is light,
And he who loveth not,
  Dwelleth in night.

Belovèd, let us love:
  For only thus
Shall we behold that God
  Who loveth us.

HORATIUS BONAR

Where God's law is, is God's love. Look at Law—it withers your very soul with its stern, inexorable face. But look at Love, or look at God's will, which means look at Love's will, and you are reassured, your heart grows strong...... "Love is the fulfilling of the law".

HENRY DRUMMOND

O Lord, my God, fountain of all true and holy love, who hast made me, and preserved me, that I might love Thee: give to Thy servant such a love, that whatsoever in Thy service may happen contrary to flesh and blood, I may not feel it; that humility may be my sanctuary, and Thy service the joy of my soul, and death itself the entrance of an eternal life, when I may live with Thee, my Strength and my Refuge, my God and everlasting Hope.

JEREMY TAYLOR

4. First Things First

But take diligent heed to do the commandment and the law, which Moses the servant of the Lord charged you, to love the Lord your God, and to walk in all his ways and to keep his commandments, and to cleave unto him, and to serve him with all your heart and with all your soul. *Joshua 22: 5*

Love is the first and the last and the strongest bond in experience. It conquers distance, outlives all changes, bears the strain of the most diverse opinions.

Joyful News

Father loved to feel that he was just "God's errand boy", or, as he also said, "like a little dog on a string, ready to go wherever the Master willed".

(A tribute to by Ernest Luff his daughter)

Master divine,
We thank Thee for all new beginnings,
For this new day
With its new opportunities of service for Thee and communion with Thee.
We thank Thee for landmarks passed
And new vistas opening ahead;
For new hope and new inspiration,
New national awakening, and new desire to serve our time and our country.

We thank Thee that, to those who love Thee,
The best is ever yet to be:
That, if we abide in Thee, we can never grow old,
For Thou, our Master, art eternally young,
Eternally radiant with the joyful energy, the freshness and buoyancy of youth. J. S. HOYLAND

5. Love fulfils Law

Let us hear the conclusion of the whole matter: Fear God, and keep his commandments; for this is the whole duty of man. *Ecclesiastes 12: 13*

Happy the heart where graces reign,
  Where love inspires the breast;
Love is the brightest of the train,
  And perfects all the rest.

'Tis love that makes our cheerful feet
  In swift obedience move;
The devils know, and tremble too;
  But Satan cannot love. ISAAC WATTS

Don't try to do people good; love them. Tagore said: 'He who tries to do people good stands knocking at the door, but he who loves them finds the door open'.
We know, ourselves, how much we resent being stalked by someone intent to do us 'good'............... But few people can resist genuine love.
So love them—with supernatural love: the love which does not run on lines of mere affinity, but loves even where it cannot like. It is a gift, of course—a gift from God; freely given to importunate prayer.
This it is that converts dry bones into living bodies, and mere forms into channels of the Spirit—the impelling force of love. W. E. SANGSTER

Show me thy ways, O Lord: teach me thy paths. Lead me in thy truth, and teach me; for thou art the God of my salvation; on thee do I wait all the day.
All the paths of the Lord are mercy and truth unto such as keep his covenant and his testimonies.
Let integrity and uprightness preserve me; for I wait on thee. *Psalm 25: 4, 5, 10, 21*

6. A Many-Splendoured Thing

He brought me to the banqueting house, and his banner over me was love. *Song of Solomon 2: 4*

Many waters cannot quench love, neither can the floods drown it: if a man would give all the substance of his house for love, it would utterly be contemned.
Song of Solomon 8: 7

Love is a great thing, yea, a great and thorough good. Nothing is sweeter than love, nothing more courageous, nothing higher, nothing more pleasant, nothing fuller nor better in heaven and earth; because love is born of God, and cannot rest but in God, above all created things. He that loveth, flieth, runneth, and rejoiceth; he is free and is not bound. Love knows no burden, thinks nothing of trouble, attempts what is above its strength, pleads no excuse of impossibility; for it thinks all things lawful for itself and all things possible.
It is therefore able to undertake all things, and it completes many things and brings them to conclusion, where he who does not love faints and lies down.
THOMAS Á KEMPIS

Immortal love, for ever full,
For ever flowing free,
For ever shared, for ever whole,
A never ebbing sea. J. G. WHITTIER

Almighty God, unto whom all hearts be open, all desires known, and from whom no secrets are hid; cleanse the thoughts of our hearts by the inspiration of Thy Holy Spirit, that we may perfectly love Thee, and worthily magnify Thy Holy name. Through Christ our Lord.
The Book of Common Prayer

7. The New Commandment

These things have I spoken unto you, that my joy might remain in you, and that your joy might be full.

John 15: 11

This is my commandment, That ye love one another, as I have loved you... Ye are my friends, if ye do whatsoever I command you... These things I command you, that ye love one another. *John 15: 12. 14. 17*

"Service is the rent we pay for our room in the world". Surely love is the highest rent in service that could be paid! And my rent should be very high, for I always have had such a lovely and beautiful room in the world—lovely Christian parents, a background of love—lovely Christian friends, a Christian husband, Christian relatives plus my personal knowledge of the Love of God—so many, many great blessings. And here I am wishing I could do this and that—go there and there, see so and so—when just where I am I can love—send up loving prayers think loving thoughts, write helpful, loving letters and do kind, loving deeds—just where I am. Yes I *must* pay a bigger rent in more love for my room in the world. *(From the diary of the compiler)*

Love shall be our token
  Love be yours and love be mine,
Love to God and all man,
  Love for plea and gift and sign.

CHRISTINA ROSSETTI

O God, pour into our hearts such love toward Thee, that we, loving Thee above all things, may obtain Thy promises, which exceed all that we can desire; through Jesus Christ our Lord. *Collect, 6th Sunday after Trinity*

8. The Chief Commandment

A lawyer asked him, Master, which is the greatest commandment in the law? Jesus said unto him, Thou shalt love the Lord thy God with all thy heart, and with all thy soul, and with all thy mind. This is the first and great commandment.
And the second is like unto it, Thou shalt love thy neighbour as thyself.
On these two commandments hang all the law and the prophets. *Matthew 22: 36–40*

A new commandment I give unto you, That ye love one another; as I have loved you, that ye also love one another. By this shall all men know that ye are my disciples, if ye have love one to another.

John 13: 34. 35

Life without love is a meaningless story.
Love is the answer, the power and the glory.
Love is the lamp on the untrodden road,
Lighting the way to the heart's true abode.

PATIENCE STRONG

A friend invited me to lunch in London to meet Sister Doreen Gemmel—a Church Army Sister working among drug addicts in the city. Love shone from her face. She told us about her work. "However do you convert them?" I asked. "I just love them," she said.

Though here our true selves may never be realized,
Yet keep and use in thine own good time our powers
for love and for goodness;
Pour them in thy secret reservoirs,
Whence all the nations of the earth,
Shall some day be refreshed and restored with thy
water of life. J. S. HOYLAND

9. Loving our Neighbour

Thou shalt love thy neighbour as thyself.

Leviticus 19: 18

And a lawyer said unto Jesus, And who is my neighbour? .... And Jesus answering said, A certain man went down from Jerusalem to Jericho, and fell among thieves, which stripped him of his raiment, and wounded him, and departed, leaving him half dead. And by chance there came down a certain priest that way: and when he saw him, he passed by on the other side. And likewise a Levite, when he was at the place, came and looked on him, and passed by on the other side. But a certain Samaritan, as he journeyed, came where he was: and when he saw him, he had compassion on him, and went to him, and bound up his wounds, pouring in oil and wine, and set him on his own beast, and brought him to an inn, and took care of him. And on the morrow when he departed, he took out two pence, and gave them to the host, and said unto him, Take care of him, and whatsoever thou spendest more, when I come again, I will repay thee. Which now of these three, thinkest thou, was neighbour unto him that fell among the thieves?

And he said, He that shewed mercy on him. Then said Jesus unto him, Go, and do thou likewise.

Luke 10: 29–37

"Love is not getting but giving; not a wild dream of pleasure and a madness of desire. Oh no! love is not that—it is goodness and honour, peace, and pure living."

Father, hear the prayer we offer;
Not for ease that prayer shall be,
But for strength that we may ever
Live our lives courageously. L. M. WILLIS

10. Love One Another

For this is the message that ye heard from the beginning, that we should love one another.
And this is his commandment, That we should believe on the name of his Son Jesus Christ, and love one another, as he gave us commandment.
And he that keepeth his commandments dwelleth in him, and he in him.
And hereby we know that he abideth in us, by the Spirit which he hath given us. *1 John 3: 11, 23, 24*

No person can heal or reform mankind unless he is actuated by love and goodwill towards men.
The life of Christ Jesus, his words and deeds, demonstrate Love.
Without love we cannot heal. This love comes only through following the Christ with all our heart.
Christian Science Sentinel

Christian love is that unbeatable good will which nothing can change to bitterness or hate.... There must come into the hearts of men what we call a new spirit: and that spirit is the Holy Spirit. The Holy Spirit not only unites men to God; He unites men to one another. Life in the Spirit is life in the conscious awareness of God; and he who is consciously aware of God can never hate. *Source Unknown*

Almighty God, from whom all thoughts of truth and peace proceed; kindle, we pray Thee, in the hearts of all men the true love of peace; and guide with Thy pure and peaceable wisdom those who take counsel for the nations of the earth; that in tranquility thy kingdom may go forward, till the earth is filled with the knowledge of thy love: through Jesus Christ our Lord. BISHOP PAGET

11. Love in Action

My children, our love is not to be just words or mere talk, but something real and active; only by this can we be certain that we are children of the truth. His commandments are these: that we believe in the name of his Son Jesus Christ and that we love one another as he told us to. Whoever keeps his commandments lives in God and God lives in him. We know that he lives in us by the Spirit that he has given us.

1 John 3: 18, 19, 23, 24 (Jerusalem Bible)

Beloved, let us love so well
Our work shall be the better for our love,
And still our love be sweeter for our work
And both commended for the sake of each,
By all true workers, and true lovers born.

E. B. BROWNING

O Love, that makes heavy burdens light,
O Love, that makest bitter things most sweet,
O Love, that robs the darkness from the night,
That resteth tired, wayworn, pilgrim feet;

Not only in the Bethlehem of old,
But in the mews and street, and at our door;
Not only in the chalice gleaming gold,
But in the patient faces of the poor.

FATHER ANDREW

O Lord God, our heavenly Father, we lift up our hearts in joy and thankfulness to Thee for the gift of Thy Son Jesus Christ, who came to show us Thy love, and to stir up our love for Thee. Fill us, O Lord, with Thy Spirit. May we always strive to keep Thy commandments, and to love one another.

12. Unconquerable Love

Who shall separate us from the love of Christ? .....
I am persuaded that neither death, nor life, nor angels, nor principalities, nor powers, nor things present, nor things to come, nor height, nor depth, nor any other creature, shall be able to separate us from the love of God, which is in Christ Jesus our Lord.

Romans 8: 35, 38, 39

I believe that love is stronger than all other forces; that to love is better than to be angry, that it is better to give than to receive, better to serve than to be served. I believe that God's kingdom CAN come on earth, and that everything that is wrong in the life of the nation, or of the Church, or in my life, can be conquered by the power of God. I believe that nothing that is wrong need be permanent. A. HERBERT GRAY

Fill me with gladness from above,
  Hold me by strength divine!
Lord, let the glow of Thy great love
  Through my whole being shine.

Make this poor self grow less and less,
  Be Thou my life and aim;
O make me daily, through Thy grace,
  More meet to bear Thy name.

JOHANN LAVATER

We thank Thee, O Lord, for all those good things which are in our world and in our lives through Thy love... Give strength of spirit to rise into joyfulness of heart. By Thy help may we learn to love as those should who have trusted the promises of good which are incarnate in Jesus, and who know that in the end love must conquer.

A. HERBERT GRAY

13. He Loved Us First

We ourselves have known and put our faith in God's love towards ourselves. God is love and anyone who lives in love lives in God, and God lives in him. Love will come to its perfection in us when we can face the day of judgement without fear; because even in this world we have become as he is. In love there can be no fear, but fear is driven out by perfect love: we are to love, then, because he loved us first.

1 John 4: 16–19 (Jerusalem Bible)

We love Him because He first loved us. God started it. No man can or will ever explain *why* God loves us. He hath loved, He hath loved us, because *He would love.* He chose to, just because He *is* love. He is such a God! Seeing the love at the heart of the universe, the saint sees the tragedy which is there also. God loves as only God *can* love, and men are heedless of it. Even when men hear of that love, they do not realise it. Love is the vital force upholding all creation and the initiative of loving is always with God. "Herein is love, not that we loved God, but that he loved us"—and the echo of Christ's words to his disciples—"You have not chosen me, but I have chosen you". W. E. SANGSTER

Let me no more my comfort draw
  From my frail hold of Thee;
In this alone rejoice with awe—
  Thy mighty grasp of me.

JOHN CAMPBELL SHARP

O my God, I believe that Thou art good and great, perfect in wisdom and in love, and that Thou lovest me.

G. A. STUDDERT-KENNEDY

14. Love within us

Beloved, let us love one another; for love is of God; and everyone that loveth is born of God, and knoweth God. He that loveth not knoweth not God; for God is love. In this was manifested the love of God toward us, because that God sent his only begotten Son into the world, that we might live through him.
Herein is love, not that we loved God, but that he loved us and sent his Son to be the propitiation for our sins. *1 John 4: 7–10*

The basis of Quaker life and practice is a conviction that there is something of God's spirit in us all; that every soul can have immediate communion with Him. It involves an attempt to accept literally the command to love God and one another. It rules out war. It recognises evil but meets it with active goodwill which outlasts it or transforms it. Such beliefs have involved sacrifice and much suffering. The Quaker way of life leads us to think of men and women all the world over as parts of the family of God. W. E. SANGSTER

The keynote of John Woolman, the Quaker saint, was ever love to God and to man. This single note runs through his life and writings like a silver thread—his deathbed had the same touching concern for suffering humanity, relieved only by the thought of the paternity of God and His love W. E. SANGSTER

Let Thy love pass
into the depth of my heart
into the heart of my prayer
into the prayer of my whole being;
so that I desert myself
and dwell more and more in Thee,
in peace, now and evermore.

ERIC MILNER-WHITE

15. The Secret of Life

No man hath seen God at any time. If we love one another, God dwelleth in us, and his love is perfected in us. *1 John 4: 12*

The First Epistle of John reminds us once again that Love is the vital force upholding all creation and that the initiative of loving is always with God.
Genesis is the first stanza in the divine love song of the ages. Love is the unbroken theme linking all the books of the Old Testament to each other and to the New. Every book in the Old Testament points forwards to the Gospels, and in them the rest of the New Testament looks back.

Bible Reading Fellowship Notes

It's not what you get, but what you give,
It's not what you make, but how you live.
It's not the years that you spend on earth,
But kindly deeds that prove your worth.
So try your best from day to day,
Faithfully serve along life's way.
Be sincere; let these not depart:
Honesty, courage, beauty from your heart.
Know the truth, and acquire the treasure
Of wisdom and mercy in greater measure.
Cheerfully give and strive to possess
Universal love and happiness.

"HUMANITY'S FRIEND"

O Lord, who hast taught us that all our doings without charity are nothing worth: send thy Holy Ghost, and pour into our hearts that most excellent gift of charity...

Collect for Quinquagesima

16. A Heart of Love

By this we know that we love the children of God, when we love God, and keep his commandments. For this is the love of God, that we keep his commandments: and his commandments are not grievous. For whatsoever is born of God overcometh the world: and this is the victory that overcometh the world, even our faith.

1 John 5: 2–4

To my God a heart of flame;
To my fellow men a heart of love;
To myself a heart of steel. St. Augustine

As the weeks, the months, the years go by, we see more and more that only one thing is necessary to be happy and to make others happy, and that one thing is not money, nor connections, nor health—it is love.

Maria von Trapp

Now let us see Thy beauty, Lord,
As we have seen before;
And by Thy beauty quicken us
To love Thee and adore.

Our every feverish mood is cooled,
And gone is every load,
When we can lose the love of self,
And find the love of God.

Benjamin Waugh

Father,
Well I know that, given one trusting heart,
Silently, unnoticed, far away,
Thy Kingdom comes:
O Father, Father, here is all my heart, my mind, my will,
For Thee. J. S. Hoyland

17. Love is the Key

Moreover we know that to those who love God, who are called according to his plan, everything that happens fits into a pattern for good. God, in his foreknowledge, chose them to bear the family likeness of his Son, that he might be the eldest of a family of many brothers.

Romans 8: 28, 29 (J. B. Phillips)

Let me assert that whatever has happened to me or will happen to me, LOVE is the reality behind the universe and is finally triumphant and victorious. Let no resentment, bitterness, cynicism, or even doubt, sour my heart against love. God is LOVE, and is seeking to dwell in me in greater and greater measure.

LESLIE D. WEATHERHEAD

It is love and love alone that makes life bearable,
Lifts it from the commonplace and makes it beautiful,
Gives to it a meaning and a motive high and fine—
Touching it with something that is more than half
divine.

The love that runs with eager feet to do the
thankless tasks—
The love that seeks for no reward, the sort of love
that asks
The chance to do a little more, but never any less.
This is the kind of love that brings the greatest
happiness.

PATIENCE STRONG

18. True Love

Let your love be a real thing, with a loathing for evil and a bent for what is good. *Romans 12: 9 (Moffatt)*

The meaning of love is not to be confused with some sentimental outpouring. Love is something much deeper than emotional bosh. Perhaps the Greek language can clear our confusion at this point. In the Greek New Testament are three words for love. The word *EROS* is a sort of aesthetic or romantic love. In the Platonic dialogue *EROS* is a yearning of the soul for the realm of the divine. The second word is *PHILIA,* a reciprocal love and the intimate affection and friendship between friends. We love those whom we like, and we love because we are loved.

The third word is *AGAPE,* understanding and creative, redemptive goodwill for all men. An overflowing love which seeks nothing in return. *AGAPE* is the love of God operating in the human heart... At this level we love men not because we like them—we love every man because God loves him. At this level we love the person who does an evil deed, although we hate the deed that he does.

MARTIN LUTHER KING

O Lord our God, give us more love, more denial of self, more likeness to Thee. Teach us that it is better to give than to receive, better to forget ourselves than to put ourselves forward, better to serve than to be waited on; and unto Thee, the God of Love, be praise and glory for ever.

ST. FRANCIS OF ASSISI

19. Creative Love

Owe no man any thing, but to love one another: for he that loveth another hath fulfilled the law.
For this, Thou shalt not commit adultery, Thou shalt not kill, Thou shalt not steal, Thou shalt not bear false witness, Thou shalt not covet; and if there be any other commandment, it is briefly comprehended in this saying, namely, Thou shalt love thy neighbour as thyself. Love worketh no ill to his neighbour: therefore love is the fulfilling of the law. *Romans 13: 8–10*

To have faith is to create; To have hope is to call down blessings; To have love is to work miracles.

DAVID GRAYSON

Our Ádorable Lord is an infinity of pure Love, unbeginning, never ceasing and for ever an overflowing ocean of meekness, sweetness, delight, blessing, goodness, patience and mercy—and all this, as so many streams breaking out of the abyss of Universal Love.

WILLIAM LAW

For the beauty of the earth,
For the beauty of the skies,
For the love which from our birth
Over and around us lies,
Gracious God, to Thee we raise
This our sacrifice of praise.

For the joy of human love,
Brother, sister, parent, child,
Friends on earth and friends above,
For all gentle thoughts and mild:
Gracious God, to Thee we raise
This our sacrifice of praise.

F. S. PIERPOINT

20. Indispensable Love

I may speak in tongues of men or of angels, but if I am without love, I am a sounding gong or a clanging cymbal. I may have the gift of prophecy, and know every hidden truth; I may have faith strong enough to move mountains; but if I have no love, I am nothing. I may dole out all I possess, or even give my body to be burnt, but if I have no love, I am none the better.
Love is patient; Love is kind and envies no one. Love is never boastful, nor conceited, nor rude; never selfish, not quick to take offence. Love keeps no score of wrongs; does not gloat over other men's sins, but delights in the truth. There is nothing love cannot face; there is no limit to its faith, its hope, its endurance.
Love will never come to an end.
In a word, there are three things that last for ever: faith, hope and love; but the greatest of them all is love. Put love first.

1 Corinthians 13: 1–8, 13; 14: 1 N.E.B.

What is the beginning? Love. What is the course?
  Love still.
What is the goal? The goal is Love on the Happy Hill.
Is there nothing else than Love, search we sky and
  earth?
There is nothing out of Love hath perpetual worth.
All things fail but only Love, all things fail or flee—
There is nothing else but Love, worthy you and me.

CHRISTINA ROSSETTI

O Lord, we know that this is the message we have learnt from the beginning, that we should love one another. Grant us this fruit of the Spirit, we beseech Thee.

21. Love Abounding

I pray that your love may abound yet more and more in knowledge and in all judgment; that ye may approve things that are excellent; that ye may be sincere and without offence till the day of Christ; being filled with the fruits of righteousness, which are by Jesus Christ, unto the glory and praise of God. *Philippians 1: 9–11*

Love. Love. Love. Most truly, more truly than you have ever dreamed, does love make the world go round. Love royally. Love is all-powerful, love is ever victorious, love can cast out a thousand ill-named demons. If you are possessed by love, you are eternally blessed, eternally happy, and you bring blessing and happiness to all around you. King's Love is infinite as the sea, and it extends to all creatures, even to the weakest and meanest —the inarticulate ones. MARION REID

Let us love sunshine, fresh air and clean, pure food, and rejoice in all the good that comes our way—the blue sky, the trees and flowers, sunrise, sunset—let us think love, be love, and love will flow back to us and make us whole and full of joy, while within us will develop latent powers of which we have never dreamed, and through which the world will be blessed. MARION REID

Love divine, all loves excelling,
Joy of heaven, to earth come down;
Fix in us Thy humble dwelling,
All Thy faithful mercies crown:
Jesu, Thou art all compassion,
Pure unbounded love Thou art:
Visit us with Thy salvation,
Enter every trembling heart.

CHARLES WESLEY

22. Make Me Like Jesus

Even as the Father hath loved me, I also have loved you: abide ye in my love. If ye keep my commandments, ye shall abide in my love; even as I have kept my Father's commandments, and abide in his love.

John 15: 9–11 (Revised Version)

We must grow as flowers in the garden of the Lord, remembering that true growth is from within outwards, and that the kingdom of God is within us—that is the whole secret. Let us live the inner life of love, and the outer life will adjust itself, and become a harmonious expression of the life within.

Where love reigns, no evil thing can exist—neither jealousy nor envy, neither hatred nor malice nor any other uncharitableness—nothing but what is good. There would be no social discord, and no wars—how could there be where all is love? The redemption of the world is by Divine Love, and that love can only work through human channels. Every woman can be, nay, HAS to be a channel through which this Divine Love may work. God calls YOU to be a King's Daughter, the daughter of the King of Love.

MARION REID

Father, we thank Thee for human love.
For Thou, O Father, art Love; and Thou art eternal!
And all pure love, loved in Thee, is for eternity.

J. S. HOYLAND

23. A Spirit Refreshed

And be renewed in the spirit of your mind; and that ye put on the new man, which after God is created in righteousness and true holiness. Wherefore putting away lying, speak every man truth with his neighbour: for we are members one of another. Be ye angry, and sin not: let not the sun go down upon your wrath: neither give place to the devil. Let him that stole steal no more: but rather let him labour, working with his hands the thing which is good, that he may have to give to him that needeth. Let no corrupt communication proceed out of your mouth, but that which is good to the use of edifying, that it may minister grace unto the hearers. And grieve not the holy Spirit of God, whereby ye are sealed unto the day of redemption. Let all bitterness, and wrath, and anger, and clamour, and evil speaking, be put away from you, with all malice: and be ye kind one to another, tenderhearted, forgiving one another, even as God for Christ's sake hath forgiven you.
Be ye therefore followers of God, as dear children; and walk in love, as Christ also hath loved us, and hath given himself for us an offering and a sacrifice to God for a sweetsmelling savour.

Ephesians 4: 23–32; 5: 1

Love, and God will pay you with the capacity for more love. For love is heaven; love is God within you.

F. W. ROBERTSON

O Love that wilt not let me go,
I rest my weary soul in Thee:
I give Thee back the life I owe,
That in Thine ocean depths its flow
May richer, fuller be.

GEORGE MATHESON

24. Helping One Another

Let us hold fast the profession of our faith without wavering; (for he is faithful that promised;) and let us consider one another to provoke unto love and to good works. *Hebrews 10: 23, 24*

When morning wakes me to a new day, may the spirit of joyous adventure quicken in me, and though my work lie amid the turmoil of cities, may the spirit of inward peace be with me. Let the spirit of joy enfold me so that I radiate happiness and like the birds lift up my head and sing. May the spirit of humour be my companion, and help me to laugh over the troubles and appreciate to the full life's simple pleasures. May the spirit of love fill me with blessings, in such an abundance that they overflow on all round me. *Source Unknown*

Like their Lord, the recipients of His love love where they do not like. It is impossible to think that Christ liked rotting lepers, bloated publicans, loose women or wild demoniacs; yet it is undeniable that He loved them. Those to whom, in response to faith, He gives this supernatural love, love in that way. It is not more of the love they had before: it is love with a new quality.

W. E. SANGSTER

Help us to help each other, Lord,
Each other's cross to bear,
Let each his friendly aid afford,
And feel his brother's care.

Help us to build each other up,
Our little stock improve:
Increase our faith, confirm our hope,
And perfect us in love.

CHARLES WESLEY

25. Love is the Spur

Knowledge puffs up, love builds up. Whoever imagines he has attained to some degree of knowledge, does not possess the true knowledge yet; but if anyone loves God, he is known by Him. *1 Corinthians 8: 1–3 (Moffatt)*

Love when true, faithful and well fixed, is eminently the sanctifying element of human life; without it the soul cannot reach its fullest height of holiness.

JOHN RUSKIN

The world is one great family of every clime and race:
We pray that all together in love may pass our days.

Come, let us join our hands in one and sing the song of peace:
Let all the world be comrades, and let our joys increase.

The seven seas of olden days are now a single one:
This world of ours must also be joined in unison.

The clouds of hatred, clouds of doubt between us must not be:
With visions bright before us, we'll work in harmony.

The world's a mighty family with hands across the seas:
The flame of love within us must burn and never cease.
(A Japanese song sheet given to the compiler in 1934.)

Ah, Lord God, Thou holy Lover of my soul, when Thou comest into my soul, all that is within me shall rejoice: being inwardly cured and thoroughly cleansed, I may be made fit to love, courageous to suffer, steady to persevere. Nothing is sweeter than Love, nothing more courageous.

THOMAS Á KEMPIS

26. Love for Enemies

I say unto you, Love your enemies, bless them that curse you, do good to them that hate you, and pray for them which despitefully use you, and persecute you; that ye may be the children of your Father which is in heaven: for he maketh his sun to rise on the evil and on the good, and sendeth rain on the just and on the unjust.

Matthew 5: 44, 45

Today I have been lent the weekend *Observer* magazine. I am impressed with the following lines: "Love your enemies, do good to them that hate you! The ethic is original. It can be isolated as Jesus' own teaching, and in nearly 2000 years it has not yet been obeyed. Was it really asking for too much? Yet today, when to hate one's enemies may entail literally the destruction of civilization, it appears more and more relevant. This strange doctrine from the strange Jewish rabbi of 2000 years ago becomes more rather than less intellectually respectable in the scientific age".

(From the diary of the compiler)

O love of God! O sin of man! In this dread act your strength is tried;
And victory remains with love: for He, our Lord, is crucified.

F. W. FABER

Thou camest, O Lord,
With the living word
That should set Thy children free;
But with mocking scorn
And with crown of thorn
They bore Thee to Calvary:
O come to my heart, Lord Jesus;
Thy Cross is my only plea.

EMILY E. S. ELLIOTT

27. God's Initiative

Herein is love, not that we loved God, but that he loved us, and sent his Son to be the propitiation for our sins.

1 John 4: 10

I go to prepare a place for you. And if I go and prepare a place for you, I will come again, and receive you unto myself; that where I am, there ye may be also.

John 14: 2–3

This, this is the God we adore,
  Our faithful, unchangeable Friend;
Whose love is as great as His power,
  And neither knows measure nor end.

'Tis Jesus, the first and the last,
  Whose Spirit shall guide us safe home;
We'll praise Him for all that is past,
  And trust Him for all that's to come.

JOSEPH HART

In everyone of us there is the ability to respond to the love of God, and to praise and trust Him.

Source unknown

Fill us, we pray Thee, with Thy light and life, that we may show forth Thy wondrous glory. Grant that Thy love may so fill our lives that we may count nothing too small to do for Thee, nothing too much to give, and nothing too hard to bear. So teach us, Lord, to serve Thee as Thou deservest, to give and not to count the cost, to fight and not to heed the wounds, to toil and not to seek for rest, to labour and not to ask for any reward save that of knowing that we do Thy will.

IGNATIUS LOYOLA

28. Our Response

That Christ may dwell in your hearts by faith; that ye, being rooted and grounded in love, may be able to comprehend with all saints what is the breadth, and length, and depth, and height; and to know the love of Christ, which passeth knowledge, that ye might be filled with all the fulness of God. *Ephesians 3: 17–19*

The whole New Testament has these two themes: on the one hand, what God offers us freely in immeasurable love demonstrated by Christ; on the other, our response in experience as life is revolutionised by love. Life is made up of contrasts—darkness and light, love and disobedience. The choice is ours, but there are no half-measures.

Bible Reading Fellowship notes

O the deep, deep love of Jesus,
  Love of every love the best:
'Tis an ocean vast of blessing,
  'Tis a haven sweet of rest,
O the deep, deep love of Jesus,
  'Tis a heaven of heavens to me;
And it lifts me up to glory,
  For it lifts me up to Thee.
O the deep, deep love of Jesus,
  Vast, unmeasured, boundless, free.

O God, Fountain of love, pour Thy love into our souls, that we may love those whom Thou lovest, with the love Thou givest us, and think and speak of them tenderly, meekly, lovingly; and so loving our brethren and sisters for Thy sake may grow in Thy love, and dwelling in love may dwell in Thee; for Jesus Christ's sake.

E. B. Pusey

29. God Uses Us

Steady then, keep cool and pray! Above all, be keen to love one another, for love hides a host of sins. Be hospitable to each other, and do not grudge it. You must serve one another, each with the talent he has received, as efficient stewards of God's varied grace.

1 Peter 4: 8–10 (Moffatt)

When any master holds
'Twixt chin and hand a violin of mine,
He will be glad that Stradivari lived,
Made violins, and made them of the best.
And while God gives them skill,
I give them instruments to play upon,
God choosing me to help Him.
If my hand slacked I should rob God,
Leaving a blank instead of violins.
'Tis God gives skill,
But not without men's hands: He could not make
Antonio Stradivari's violins
Without Antonio.

GEORGE ELIOT

O Loving Lord, who art for ever seeking
Men of Thy mind, intent to do Thy will,
Strong in Thy strength, Thy power and grace bespeaking,
Faithful to Thee, through good report and ill;

Not disobedient to the heavenly vision.
Faithful in all things, seeking not reward,
Then, following Thee, may we fulfil our mission,
True to ourselves, our brethren, and our Lord. Amen.

WILLIAM VAUGHAN JENKINS

30. Liking and Loving

Thou shalt love thy neighbour as thyself: I am the Lord.
Leviticus 19: 18

Love is the greatest thing that God can give us, for He Himself is love, and it is the greatest thing we can give to God, for it will also give ourselves, and carry with it all that is ours. *Source unknown*

At this level we can see what Jesus meant when He said, 'Love your enemies'... We should be happy that He did not say, 'Like your enemies'. 'Like' is a sentimental and affectionate word... How can we like a person who is threatening our children and bombing our homes? That is impossible. But Jesus recognised that 'love' is greater than 'like'. When Jesus bids us to love our enemies, He is speaking neither of *eros,* nor *philia:* He is speaking of *agape,* understanding and creative, redemptive goodwill for all men. Only by following this way, and responding with this type of love, are we able to be children of our Father who is in heaven.
MARTIN LUTHER KING

Immortal Love, for ever full
For ever flowing free,
For ever shared, for ever whole,
A never-ebbing sea.
J. G. WHITTIER

Almighty God, giver of those gifts which enable us to do Thy will, grant unto us, Thy children, faith, devotion, understanding and love. Lead us into all truth, and may we ever grow in grace, and love for Thee and our neighbour, and become truer followers of Jesus Christ our Lord.

SECTION TWO – The Lord thy God

31. Te Deum Laudamus

O Lord our Lord, how excellent is thy name in all the earth! *Psalm 8: 1*

We praise Thee, O God: we acknowledge Thee to be
the Lord.
All the earth doth worship Thee: the Father
everlasting.
To Thee all angels cry aloud: the heavens, and all
the powers therein.
To Thee cherubin and seraphin continually do cry,
Holy, holy, holy: Lord God of Sabaoth;
Heaven and earth are full of the majesty of Thy glory.
The glorious company of the apostles praise Thee.
The goodly fellowship of the prophets praise Thee.
The noble army of martyrs praise Thee:
The holy Church throughout all the world doth
acknowledge Thee:
The Father of an infinite majesty; Thine honourable,
true and only Son:
Also the Holy Ghost, the Comforter.

Te Deum Laudamus

I dwell in thought upon the amazing truth that God loves me! As His child I am a member of the royal family of the King of Heaven. This love encircles the world, and within this circle I am related to every member of the human family.

PATIENCE STRONG

O Lord, Thy majesty and glory fill us with praise and thanksgiving, as we realize that we are Thy children and that each one of us is loved by Thee. Accept our love, O Lord, and our service.

32. Creator

In the beginning God created the heaven and the earth.
And God said, Let there be light; and there was light,
And God saw the light that it was good.

Genesis 1: 3, 4

The spacious firmament on high,
With all the blue ethereal sky,

And spangled heavens, a shining frame,
Their great Original proclaim.

JOSEPH ADDISON

Before the world or man was, God IS. And for us that means not ineffable, unsullied splendour, but that his very nature is love reaching out; it is an essential part of the gospel we preach that the creation itself is the fruit of God's love.

T. J. FOINETTE

Master Divine,
Keep us and guard us this day,
Fill our souls with the light of Thy presence:
Guard us from shame and from night:
Girdle us round with Thy heavenly defences,
That the citadel of our hearts may be inviolate.

Vouchsafe unto us Thy Spirit,
That we be clothed in Thine armour of light,
Worthy of our place in Thine armies,
Strong to fight gallantly for Thee,
Faithful till death beyond death,
Secure for all eternity in Thy leadership and Thy love.

J. S. HOYLAND

33. God in Everything

And God said, Let there be a firmament in the midst of the waters, and let it divide the waters from the waters. And God called the firmament Heaven. And God said, Let the waters under the heavens be gathered together unto one place, and let the dry land appear: and it was so. And God called the dry land Earth; and the gathering together of the waters called he Seas. And God saw that it was good. *Genesis 1: 6, 8–10*

O worship the King,
All glorious above; O gratefully sing
His power and His love;
Our shield and defender, the ancient of days,
Pavilioned in splendour, and girded with praise.

The earth with its store of wonders untold,
Almighty! Thy power hath founded of old,
Hath stablished it fast by a changeless decree,
And round it hath cast, like a mantle, the sea.

ROBERT GRANT

A patronising cynic saw a boy leaving his Sunday School one afternoon. Thinking to score a cheap victory over the youngster, he said to the lad, "Look here, son, you've just come from Sunday School, haven't you? Well, I'll give you an apple if you'll tell me where God is". Quick as a flash came the inspired answer: "And I'll give you a barrel if you can tell me where God isn't".

My God I thank Thee, who hast made the earth so bright,
So full of splendour and of joy, beauty and light;
So many glorious things are here, noble and right.

ADELAIDE ANNE PROCTER

34. God and Nature

And God said, Let the earth bring forth grass, the herb yielding seed, and the fruit tree yielding fruit after his kind, whose seed is in itself, upon the earth: and it was so. And God saw that it was good. *Genesis 1: 11, 12*

I sing the almighty power of God
  That made the mountains rise,
That spread the flowing seas abroad
  And built the lofty skies.

I sing the goodness of the Lord
  That filled the earth with food;
He formed the creatures with his word
  And then pronounced them good.

ISAAC WATTS

As the art of life is learned it will be found at last that all lovely things are also necessary; the wild flowers by the wayside, as well as the tended corn; and the wild birds and creatures of the forest as well as the tended cattle; because man doth not live by bread only but also by the desert manna; by every work of God.

JOHN RUSKIN

O Lord of every lovely thing,
  The Maker of them all,
Who from the winter's gloomy wing
Doth shed the splendours of the Spring,
  On Thy great name we call.

With songs of love our hearts inspire,
  The mighty love of God.

ROBERT CALLIN

35. Light

And God made two great lights; the greater light to rule the day, and the lesser light to rule the night: he made the stars also. And God set them in the firmament of the heaven to give light upon the earth, and to rule over the day and over the night, and to divide the light from darkness: and God saw that it was good.

Genesis 1: 16–18

How valuable light is to us... in many and varied ways. How *important* too. Elderlies have the recollection of the thick black curtains at the windows in the war days (especially those of us who lived near important targets—for then light could mean loss of life!) Spring sunshine comes showing up any dark shabby places in our homes... time for a Spring Clean! Stars, what a joy! This week there is one solitary star beaming in the skies as I walk home in the darkness, giving me joy. No wonder that God saw that it was good. Thank God for the light—and above all for his gift of Jesus the Light of the World.

The unwearied sun, from day to day,
Doth his Creator's power display;
And publishes to every land
The work of an almighty hand.

J. ADDISON

There is no darkness so great that it will put out a little light.

Let my bearing today, O Lord, carry out and express the affirmation I make of Thy love. Forbid that any grumbling, self-pity or criticism of others should darken the pathway which others have to tread. Let my impact on others be that of light and love, and do Thou, by Thine inflowing love, lighten the darkness within me.

LESLIE D. WEATHERHEAD

36. Genesis

And God said, Let the waters bring forth abundantly the moving creature that hath life, and fowl that may fly above the earth in the open firmament of heaven. And God created great whales, and every living creature that moveth, which the waters brought forth abundantly, after their kind, and every winged fowl, after his kind: and God saw that it was good. And God blessed them, saying, Be fruitful and multiply, and fill the waters in the seas, and let fowl multiply in the earth. *Genesis 1: 20–22*

Genesis (its Hebrew name is *Bereshith*) means 'in the beginning'. An appropriate designation.... represented by one Greek manuscript, 'The Book of Origins'... It is a collection of the earliest traditions of the Israelites regarding the beginning of things, and particularly of their national history; these traditions being woven into a continuous narrative, commencing with the creation of the world and ending with the death of Joseph.

From a Concordance

Praise to the living God!
All praisèd be His name....
Established is His law,
And changeless it shall stand,
Deep writ upon the human heart,
On sea, on land.

Jewish Doxology (Mediaeval)

Lord of all life, life of the Past, the Now, and the Hereafter, we (Thy older children) offer our heartfelt thanks for Thy manifold blessings and abundant mercies over the long years that are past. For the years that remain, grant us Thy gifts of tranquility of mind and contented hearts. May we be an influence for peace in the lives of others. WINIFRED ADAIR-ROBERTS, QUAKER

37. God and Man

And God said, Let us make man in our image, after our likeness: and let them have dominion over the fish of the sea, and over the fowl of the air, and over the cattle, and over all the earth, and over every creeping thing that creepeth upon the earth.
So God created man in his own image, in the image of God created he him; male and female created he them.
And God blessed them, and God said unto them, Be fruitful, and multiply and replenish the earth, and subdue it; and have dominion over the fish of the sea, and over the fowl of the air, and over every living thing that moveth upon the earth.
And God saw everything that he had made, and, behold, it was very good. *Genesis 1: 26–28, 31*

Let all the world in every corner sing:
My God and King!
    The heavens are not too high,
    His praise may thither fly;
    Thc carth is not too low,
    His praises there may grow.
Let all the world in every corner sing:
My God and King!

GEORGE HERBERT

God is greater, more loving, nearer and more available for our help and comfort than any man has ever dreamed.

W. H. FINDLAY

Almighty God, who hast created man in Thine own image, grant us fearlessly to contend against evil and to make no peace with oppression, through Jesus Christ our Lord.

38. The Sabbath

Thus the heavens and the earth were finished, and all the host of them. And on the seventh day God ended his work which he had made; and he rested on the seventh day from all his work which he had made. And God blessed the seventh day and sanctified it: because that in it he had rested from all his work which God created and made. *Genesis 2: 1–3*

O day of rest and gladness,
O day of joy and light,
O balm of care and sadness,
Most beautiful, most bright!
On thee the high and lowly,
Through ages joined in tune,
Sing: Holy, holy, holy,
To the great God Triune.

CHRISTOPHER WORDSWORTH

Light of light, enlighten me,
Now anew the day is dawning;
Sun of grace, the shadows flee,
Brighten Thou my Sabbath morning;
With Thy joyous sunshine blest,
Happy is my day of rest!

Fount of all our joy and peace,
To Thy living waters lead me;
Thou from earth my soul release,
And with grace and mercy feed me;
Bless Thy word that it may prove
Rich in fruits that Thou dost love.

BENJAMIN SCHMOLCK

39. Harvest

And the Lord said in his heart...... While the earth remaineth, seedtime and harvest, and cold and heat, and summer and winter, and day and night shall not cease.

Genesis 8: 21, 22

Sing to the Lord of harvest,
  Sing songs of love and praise;
With joyful hearts and voices
  Your hallelujahs raise.
By Him the rolling seasons
  In fruitful order move;
Sing to the Lord of harvest
  A song of happy love.

J. S. B. MONSELL

The time to disbelieve in a general providence watching over this universe will come when seedtime and harvest fail; when the sun is blotted out from the sky; when children are begotten and bring no protective love in the hearts of their mothers; when rain no longer falls to irrigate the parched earth; when disease is the rule and not the exception; when men lose the power of sleep, that blessed providence of nature in which we get both our courage and our strength...... But while the sun is there, and the gentle rain, the fecund earth, and all the melting loveliness of hill and vale and tree and flower; while mother-love is discoverable at every level of our social life, and all the constant forces of the world are on our side, then let us believe in the general providence of God.

W. E. SANGSTER

I will praise thee, O Lord, among the people: and I will sing praises unto thee among the nations. For thy mercy is great above the heavens: and thy truth reacheth unto the clouds.

Psalm 108: 3–4

40. Forward in God's Name

Moses my servant is dead; now therefore arise... have not I commanded thee? Be strong and of a good courage; be not afraid, neither be thou dismayed: for the Lord thy God is with thee whithersoever thou goest.

Joshua 1: 2, 9

One evening in 1938 I was preparing a talk on the text above. As I read the chapter, three words 'hit' me: *'Now therefore arise'*.

On the previous day I had been asked to become the President of the revived Weymouth branch of the National British Women's Total Abstinence Union, and had definitely refused. At once I 'phoned the National Organiser. 'Have you found a President?' 'No.' So I accepted the task.

The war came; we moved into the town and being very concerned about the welfare of the servicemen stationed in the district, I called a meeting. The Vicar of St.John's offered his Mission Hall which, as President of the N.B.W.T.A.U., I joyfully accepted... The 'B.W. Club for H.M. Forces' served on the average two thousand men and girls a day—open all and every day between 1940–1945.

What joy and blessing this 'home-from-home' gave to countless service men and girls (and to the 250 wonderful Christian voluntary helpers who risked the bombs often to be on duty). God greatly blessed the work and how thankful I am that I heard the voice—and obeyed.

Forth in Thy name, O Lord, I go,
My daily labour to pursue,
Thee, only Thee, resolved to know
In all I think, or speak, or do.

CHARLES WESLEY

41. God is Faithful

Know therefore that the Lord thy God, he is God, the faithful God, which keepeth covenant and mercy with them that love him and keep his commandments to a thousand generations. *Deuteronomy 7: 9*

My God, I love Thee—not because
  I hope for heaven thereby,
Nor yet because who love Thee not
  Are lost eternally.

Not with the hope of gaining aught;
  Not seeking a reward;
But as Thyself hast loved me,
  O ever-loving Lord.

E'en so I love Thee, and will love,
  And in Thy praise will sing;
Because Thou art my loving God
  And my eternal King.

FRANCIS XAVIER

Lord, give us hearts never to forget Thy love; but to dwell therein whatever we do, whether we sleep or wake, live or die, or rise again to the life that is to come. For Thy love is eternal life and everlasting rest; for this is life eternal, to know Thee and Thy infinite goodness. O let its flame never be quenched in our hearts; let it grow and brighten, till our whole souls are glowing and shining with its light and warmth. For happy are we if we continue in the love wherewith Thou hast loved us; holy are we when we love Thee steadfastly. Therefore, O Thou, whose name and essence is love, enkindle our hearts, enlighten our understandings, sanctify our wills, and fill all the thoughts of our hearts, for Jesus Christ's sake. Amen.

JOHANN ARNDT

42. The Law of God

God spake these words, and said: I am the Lord thy God: Thou shalt have none other gods but Me.

Thou shalt not make to thyself any graven image, nor the likeness of any thing that is in heaven above, or in the earth beneath, or in the water under the earth. Thou shalt not bow down to them, nor worship them: for I the Lord thy God am a jealous God, and visit the sins of the fathers upon the children unto the third and fourth generation of them that hate Me, and show mercy unto thousands in them that love Me and keep My commandments.

Thou shalt not take the name of the Lord thy God in vain: for the Lord will not hold him guiltless that taketh His name in vain.

Remember that thou keep holy the Sabbath-day. Six days shalt thou labour, and do all that thou hast to do; but the seventh day is the Sabbath of the Lord thy God. In it thou shalt do no manner of work, thou, and thy son, and thy daughter, thy man-servant, and thy maid-servant, thy cattle, and the stranger that is within thy gates. For in six days the Lord made heaven and earth, the sea, and all that in them is, and rested the seventh day: wherefore the Lord blessed the seventh day, and hallowed it.

Honour thy father and thy mother; that thy days may be long in the land which the Lord thy God giveth thee.

Thou shalt do no murder.

Thou shalt not commit adultery. Thou shalt not steal.

Thou shalt not bear false witness against thy neighbour.

Thou shalt not covet thy neighbour's house, thou shalt not covet thy neighbour's wife, nor his servant, nor his maid, nor his ox, nor his ass, nor any thing that is his.

Exodus 20: 1–17 (Prayer Book Version)

43. What is Man?

When I consider thy heavens, the work of thy fingers, the moon and the stars, which thou hast ordained; what is man, that thou are mindful of him? and the son of man that thou visitest him? For thou hast made him a little lower than the angels, and hast crowned him with glory and honour. Thou madest him to have dominion over the works of thy hands; thou hast put all things under his feet. *Psalm 8: 3–6*

Sing praise to God who reigns above,
  The God of all creation,
The God of power, the God of love,
  The God of our salvation;
With healing balm my soul He fills,
  And every faithless murmur stills:
To God all praise and glory. J. J. SCHULTZ

Our sense of the immensity of space has been increased, rather than diminished, by journeys to the moon. By comparison man seems of no significance at all. Standing at the top of a high building you can see people walking along looking like ants. Man seems insignificant until you remember that the building upon which you stand was devised in the mind of a man and built by the hands of men. Man has been put in a position of responsibility over everything else. And one day man will have to answer to God for the way he has discharged his responsibility.

International Bible Reading Association
Daily Notes

My God, my King, Thy praise I sing,
  My heart is all Thine own;
My highest powers, my choicest hours,
  I yield to Thee alone. H. F. LYTE

44. God in the Psalms

The heavens declare the glory of God; and the firmament showeth his handywork. The law of the Lord is perfect, converting the soul: the testimony of the Lord is sure, making wise the simple. The statutes of the Lord are right, rejoicing the heart: the commandment of the Lord is pure, enlightening the eyes. The fear of the Lord is clean, enduring for ever: the judgements of the Lord are true and righteous altogether. *Psalm 19: 1, 7–9*

Mercy and truth are met together; righteousness and peace have kissed each other. Truth shall spring out of the earth; and righteousness shall look down from heaven. Yea, the Lord shall give that which is good; and our land shall yield her increase. *Psalm 85: 10–12*

The Psalms are both poetry and devotion. They have been treasured by Israel and by the Christian Church alike as the greatest devotional writings, representing man's response to God and joyous celebration of all His works. They were written as a means of individual reflection and also for use in the worship of the people of God. They explore the secret places of the human heart and also summon all creation to adoration of God. In them the character of God is clearly seen in His holiness, power, mercy and righteousness.

International Bible Reading Association Daily Notes

Thank you, dear Lord, for the Book of Psalms, and for those who wrote them down, delivered them, and those too, who have been the means of our having them now. Thank you that we can read them and remember them, and for all the comfort and help they give to us. May we pass them on to others, that they may be blessed and helped, and draw near unto Thee.

45. The Lord, he is God

The earth is the Lord's, and the fulness thereof; the world, and they that dwell therein.
For he hath founded it upon the seas, and established it upon the floods. Who shall ascend into the hill of the Lord? or who shall stand in his holy place? He that hath clean hands, and a pure heart; who hath not lifted up his soul unto vanity, nor sworn deceitfully. He shall receive the blessing from the Lord, and righteousness from the God of his salvation. Lift up your heads, O ye gates; and be ye lift up, ye everlasting doors; and the King of glory shall come in. Who is this King of glory? The Lord of hosts, he is the King of glory.

Psalm 24: 1, 2, 5, 7, 10

Let all the earth in every corner sing: My God and King!
The heavens are not too high,
His praise may thither fly;
The earth is not too low,
His praises there may grow.
Let all the world in every corner sing: My God and King!

Let all the world in every corner sing: My God and King!
The church with psalms must shout,
No door can keep them out:
But, above all, the heart
Must bear the longest part.
Let all the world in every corner sing: My God and King!

GEORGE HERBERT

Create in me a clean heart, O God; and renew a right spirit within me.

Psalm 51: 10

46. Praising God (1)

O sing unto the Lord a new song; for he hath done marvellous things. Make a joyful noise unto the Lord, all the earth; make a loud noise, and rejoice and sing praise... Let the sea roar, and the fulness thereof; the world and they that dwell therein. Let the floods clap their hands; let the hills be joyful together before the Lord: for he cometh to judge the earth: with righteousness shall he judge the world, and the people with equity. *Psalm 98: 1, 4, 7–9*

Praise, my soul, the King of heaven,
  To His feet thy tribute bring;
Ransomed, healed, restored, forgiven,
  Who like thee His praise should sing?
    Praise Him! Praise Him!
Praise the everlasting King.

Father Fatherlike He tends and spares us;
  Well our feeble frame He knows;
In His hands He gently bears us,
  Rescues us from all our foes:
    Praise Him! Praise Him!
Widely as His mercy flows.

H. F. LYTE

(This hymn was sung at the wedding of Queen Elizabeth II)

Rejoice the soul of thy servant; for unto thee, O Lord, do I lift up my soul. For thou, Lord, art good, and ready to forgive; and plenteous in mercy unto all them that call upon thee... In the day of my trouble I will call upon thee: for thou wilt answer me... For thou art great, and doest wondrous things: thou art God alone.

Psalm 86: 4, 5, 7, 10

47. Praising God (2)

Make a joyful noise unto the Lord, all ye lands. Serve the Lord with gladness: come before his presence with singing. Enter into his gates with thanksgiving, and into his courts with praise; be thankful unto him, and bless his name. For the Lord is good; his mercy is everlasting.

Psalm 100: 1, 2, 4, 5

The Hebrew name for the book of Psalms is *Tehillim,* meaning Songs of Praise. One can hardly miss the joyousness of their worship as we read the psalms... we hear the temple courts resound with praise.

International Bible Reading Association Notes

A gladsome hymn of praise we sing,
And thankfully we gather,
To bless the love of God above,
Our everlasting Father.

A. N. BLATCHFORD

And I said to the man who stood at the gate of the year: 'Give me a light that I may tread safely into the unknown.' And he replied: 'Go out into the darkness and put your hand into the hand of God. That shall be to you better than light and safer than a known way.'
(The message King George VI gave to the nation on Christmas Day 1939).

M. LOUISE HASKINS

God of my life, through all my days
My grateful powers shall sound Thy praise;
My song shall wake with opening light,
And cheer the dark and silent night.

P. DODDRIDGE

48. The Presence of God

Whither shall I go from thy spirit? or whither shall I flee from thy presence? If I ascend up into heaven, thou art there: if I make my bed in hell, behold, thou art there. If I take the wings of the morning and dwell in the uttermost parts of the sea; even there shall thy hand lead me, and thy right hand shall hold me.
If I say, Surely the darkness shall cover me; even the night shall be light about me. Yea, the darkness hideth not from thee; but the night shineth as the day: the darkness and the light are both alike to thee.

Psalm 139: 7–12

You can find God anywhere if you learn to look for Him with the seeing eyes. The power of God can only prevail when man reaches out to lay hold of it, but there is no limit to what can happen when man does that.

F. YEATS BROWN

The Power of God comes to meet the faith that ventures out.

Source unknown

Dear Lord,
Help me to live this day
Quietly, easily;
To lean upon Thy great strength
Trustfully, restfully;
To wait the unfolding of Thy will
Patiently, joyfully;
To face tomorrow
Confidently, courageously.

(Sent to Margaret Harwood of the "Methodist Recorder" by a 95 year-old reader)

49. Blessed Assurance

The Lord is gracious, and full of compassion; slow to anger and of great mercy. The Lord is good to all: and his tender mercies are over all his works. The Lord upholdeth all that fall, and raiseth up all those that be bowed down. The Lord is righteous in all his ways, and holy in all his works. The Lord is nigh unto all them that call upon him . . . in truth. He will fulfil the desire of them that fear him: he also will hear their cry, and will save them. My mouth shall speak the praise of the Lord: and let all flesh bless his holy name for ever and ever.

Psalm 145: 8, 9, 14, 17–19, 21

Yes, God is good—in earth and sky,
From ocean depths and spreading wood,
Ten thousand voices seem to cry:
God made us all, and God is good.

Yes, God is good, all nature says,
By God's own hand with speech endued;
And man, in louder notes of praise,
Should sing for joy that God is good.

John Hampden Gurney

In God's love we find an answer to the restless thought: and we find the peace for which our weary minds have sought. In the silence we are quietened by a touch divine—When we bow our heads and say, Not my will, Lord, but Thine.

Patience Strong

O God, whose wisdom ordained the sun to rule the day, and the moon and the stars to shine by night; and whose goodness fills the earth with food, we praise Thy glorious name and give Thee thanks.

50. Hallelujah!

Praise ye the Lord. Praise the Lord, O my soul. While I live I will sing praises unto my God while I have any being. *Psalm 146: 1, 2*

(Psalm 146 is the Crusade Psalm of the World Women's Christian Temperance Union.)

The word "praise" is translated in the margin [of the Bible] by that magnificent marching word of the Hebrews, Hallelujah: so that the more correct rendering would be—Hallelujah to the Lord. If we put our trust in God, happy are we; the 'princes' and the 'Son of Man' shall yet do His will so that His kingdom shall come upon the earth, and He will not always suffer it to be unredeemed. We have a "sure word of testimony", so we fight "not as one that beateth the air". "We know in whom we have believed".

The word "help" in the third verse is more literally translated "salvation", and as the keynote of the Crusade army is Hallelujah, so is its key word Salvation. It is not help alone we seek to give, for help is often both inadequate, and temporary, but salvation *saves;* salvation knows no palliatives; salvation is high as the hope of a saint and deep as the depths of a drunkard's despair.

FRANCES E. WILLARD
(Founder of the W.W.C.T.U.)

O God, may all within me praise Thee and love Thee: for all.... Thou hast forgiven, and for all that Thou hast given; for Thine unknown blessings... for any and every gift of nature or of grace; for my power of loving; for all blessings within and without; for all that Thou hast yet in store for me; for everything whereby Thou hast drawn me to Thyself, whether joy or sorrow.

E. B. PUSEY

51. The Greatness of God

Let earth praise the Lord: sea-monsters and all the deeps, fire and hail, snow and mist, gales that obey his decree, mountains and hills, orchards and forests, wild animals and farm animals, snakes and birds, all kings on earth and nations, princes, all rulers in the world, young men and girls, old people and children too! Let them all praise the name of the Lord, for his name and no other is sublime. *Psalm 148: 7–13 (Jerusalem Bible)*

As the marsh hen secretly builds on the watery sod,
Behold I will build me a nest on the greatness of God:
By so many roots as the marsh-grass sends in the sod
I will heartily lay me a hold on the greatness of God.

SIDNEY LANIER

This, this is the God we adore,
  Our faithful unchangeable Friend;
Whose love is as great as His power
  And neither knows measure nor end.

JOSEPH HART

The peace of God passes all understanding, much more all expression. It comes down upon the soul, and makes it ring with unutterable joy and language stops. So his prayer changes into praise. He is too full to speak, so his heart bursts into song.

HENRY DRUMMOND

All things praise Thee; round her zones
Earth, with her ten thousand tones,
Rolls a ceaseless choral strain;
Roaring wind and deep-voiced main,
Rustling leaf and humming bee,
All things praise Thee: Lord, may we.

G. W. CONDER

52. God is Reliable

Hast thou not known? hast thou not heard, that the everlasting God, the Lord, the Creator of the ends of the earth, fainteth not, neither is weary? There is no searching of his understanding.
He giveth power to the faint; and to them that have no might he increaseth strength. Even the youths shall faint and be weary, and the young men shall utterly fall: but they that wait upon the Lord shall renew their strength; they shall mount up with wings as eagles; they shall run, and not be weary; and they shall walk, and not faint. *Isaiah 40: 28–31*

God! Oh! to compass the word—who tries? God, Omnipotent, Almighty, Omniscient—everywhere. And Oh, wonder of wonders, my Lord and my God; say it—venture out on the great trackless ocean and find the waves as firm to tread upon as the rocks of Galilee. Heed not storms nor boisterous billows. Jesus is just on before; sing!

GENERAL WILLIAM BOOTH

Praise to the living God!
All praisèd be His name.
Who was, and is, and is to be,
For aye the same.
Eternal life hath He
Implanted in the soul;
His love shall be our strength and stay,
While ages roll.

JEWISH DOXOLOGY (MEDIAEVAL),
Translated by Max Landsberg

O Lord, we thank Thee that we KNOW Thy promises are sure and steadfast. May we upon Thy power utterly depend.

53. God is Love

For God so loved the world, that he gave his only begotten Son, that whosoever believeth in him should not perish, but have everlasting life. *John 3: 16*

In Jesus Christ we see the love of God in action.
International Bible Reading Association Daily Notes

O Love, of whom is truth and light,
The Word and Spirit, life and power,
O Love, who thus hast bound me fast,
Beneath that gentle yoke of Thine:
Love, who hast conquered me at last,
And rapt away this heart of mine.
O Love, I give myself to Thee,
Thine ever, only Thine to be.

JOHANN SCHEFFLER

Love ever gives—and forgives; such is Love's prerogative. To the Hebrews, their God was God Almighty, the creator of all things. He sent prophets to proclaim Him. Then He gave His only Son to the World, to show what He was really like.
God is Almighty, Omniscient, Omnipresent—yet our Father, and above all He is Love, and wants *our* love.

Come, let us all unite and sing—God is love! O tell to earth's remotest bound, in Christ is full redemption found—God is love! HOWARD KINGSBURY

O Lord God, the wonder of it! Thou the God of all the earth... Creator... Father Everlasting—yet Thou lovest me! *Thou gavest Jesus Christ to the world to show us Thy love and that our love is needed in the world too. Our hearts are full of thanksgiving, O Lord, to Thee and we praise Thy holy Name.*

54. Rest in the Lord

For with God nothing shall be impossible. *Luke 1:* 37

And we know that all things work together for good to them that love God, to them who are the called according to his purpose. *Romans 8: 28*

In the castle of my soul there is a little postern gate
Where, when I enter, I am in the presence of God.
In a moment, in a turning of a thought, I am where God is.
When I meet God there, all life gains a new meaning,
Small things become great, and great things small,
Lowly and despised things are shot through with glory.
My troubles seem but the pebbles of the road,
My joys seem like the everlasting hills,
All my fever is gone in the great peace of God,
And I pass through the door from Time into Eternity.

W. RAUSCHENBUSCH

I rest me here
Without a fear —
By Thee shall all be given
That I can need,
O Friend indeed,
For this life or for heaven.
O make me true,
My heart renew,
My soul and flesh deliver!
Lord, hear my prayer,
And in Thy care
Keep me in peace for ever.

J. MAGDEBURG

55. Strong Deliverer

If God be for us, who can be against us? He that spared not his own Son, but delivered him up for us all, how shall he not with him also freely give us all things?

Romans 8: 31. 32

Immortal, invisible, God only wise,
In light inaccessible hid from our eyes,
Most blessèd, most glorious, the Ancient of Days,
Almighty, victorious, Thy great name we praise.

To all life Thou givest—to both great and small;
In all life Thou livest, the true life of all;
We blossom and flourish as leaves on the tree,
And wither and perish—but naught changeth Thee.
All laud we would render; O help us to see:
'Tis only the splendour of light hideth Thee.

WALTER CHALMERS SMITH

To God be the glory: great things He hath done!
So loved He the world that he gave us His Son;
Why yielded His life an atonement for sin,
And opened the Life gate that all may go in.
O come to the Father, through Jesus the Son:
And give Him the glory: great things He hath done!

FRANCES VAN ALSTYNE

O Lord our heavenly Father, Almighty and everlasting God, who hast safely brought us to the beginning of this day; Defend us in the same with Thy mighty power; and grant that this day we fall into no sin, neither run into any kind of danger, but that all our doings may be ordered by Thy governance, to do always that is righteous in Thy sight, through Jesus Christ our Lord.

The Collect for Grace,
Book of Common Prayer

56. Comforter

As one whom his mother comforteth, so will I comfort you. *Isaiah 66: 13*

Blessed be God, even the Father of our Lord Jesus Christ, the Father of mercies, and the God of all comfort; Who comforteth us in all our tribulation, that we may be able to comfort them which are in any trouble by the comfort wherewith we are comforted of God.
2 Corinthians 1: 3.4

The God of all comfort, the God from whom every kind of comfort comes... I can be like a child that looks up into his mother's face, and in her loving arms forgets his griefs and fears. God can be strangely near in every time of special need, and giving to me...an increasing sense that I am not taking this journey alone... And sometimes in some flash of inward awareness He makes me see clearly, lifts the burden and turns my sorrow into song. It may be that today my personal troubles are almost forgotten in a crushing sense of the world's sorrow, but let me listen. He bids me lift up my eyes, and see God at work in this world, His own hopes undiscouraged. FRANCIS B. JAMES

On the future, once so dark, the light of hope is shed —
And the promise is fulfilled; they shall be comforted.
FROM A PATIENCE STRONG VERSE

My God....make me so sure of Thee that some who know me shall find in my fellowship the assurance of Thy love. Make my hands steady in Thy strength to guide and uphold, make them tender with Thy tenderness to soothe and help. Dwell in my heart for my own healing, and live in my life that others may be blessed, O God of all comfort. FRANCIS B. JAMES

57. Dwelling in Love

And we have known and believed the love that God hath to us. God is love; and he that dwelleth in love dwelleth in God, and God in Him. *1 John 4: 16*

Come, let us all unite and sing —
God is love!
While heaven and earth their praises bring —
God is love!
Let every soul from sin awake,
Each in his heart sweet music make,
God is love!

How happy is our portion here —
God is love!
His promises our spirits cheer —
God is love!
He is our sun and shield by day,
By night He near our tents will stay,
He will be with us all the way —
God is love!

HOWARD KINGSBURY

There is no place where God is not; Wherever I go, there God is. Now and always He upholds me with His power, and keeps me safe in His love.

Source unknown

O God, Thou lovest these souls that we love with a love as far surpassing our own, as the glory of noon surpasses the gleam of a candle. Therefore will we be still and trust in Thee.

J. S. HOYLAND

58. The Shepherd

The Lord is my shepherd, I shall not want.

Psalm 23: 1

The Great Father above a Shepherd Chief is. I am His and with Him I want not. He throws out to me a rope and the name of the rope is love, and he draws me to where the grass is green and the water is not dangerous, and I eat and lie down and am satisfied. Sometimes my heart is very weak and falls down, but He lifts me up again and draws me into a good road. His name is WONDERFUL. Sometime, it may be very soon, it may be a long, long, time, He will draw me into a valley. It is dark there, but I'll be afraid not, for it is between these mountains that the Shepherd Chief will meet me and the hunger that I have in my heart all through this life will be satisfied. Sometimes He makes the love rope into a whip, but afterwards He gives me a staff to lean upon. He spreads a table before me with all kinds of foods. He puts his hand upon my head and all the "tired" is gone. My cup fills until it runs over. What I tell is true. I lie not. These roads that are "away ahead" will stay with me through this life and after; and afterwards I will go to live in the big Tepee and sit down with the Shepherd Chief forever.
(A beautiful Canadian Indian version of the Twenty-third Psalm which was translated into a universal sign language for neighbouring tribes who spoke different dialects. A missionary then re-translated it into literal English—Indian style.)

Lord, we pray for Thy children all over the world—in every nation wherever they are... May all learn of Thy great Love for them as pictured in this beautiful Psalm of David.

59. A Father's Love

Keep yourselves in the love of God. *Jude 21*

The giant trees reached up 200 feet to form a leafy roof through which the beams of sunlight rarely penetrated. Trailing creepers hung down to meet the dense undergrowth. Mile after mile we went without being able to see the skyline. Only once during that morning did we see any sign of human life, so shy are the pygmies and other dwellers in the Ituri Forest. It was all very strange and somehow we felt further from home than we had ever done before.

At last we came to a small clearing where a missionary and his wife lived in order to make contact with the forest people, for Christ's sake. Around the house, with its doors and windows necessarily screened against the thousand and one flying insects, was a thick band of butterflies, dull brown ones, knee-deep, which flew up in a choking, fluttering cloud when we pushed into them to get to the door.

It was all rather weird and off-putting with the overall sense of being shut in by the great trees.

But there was nothing strange about the welcome we received from the elderly Scottish couple who gladly shared their simple lunch with us and we shall never forget the manner and tone in which the Rev. John Dean began his grace with the word: "Father, ...".

He need not have said anything else! With that one word, in the way he spoke it, loneliness, fear and weakness, were dismissed. God—our loving, unfailing, onward-leading Father—was suddenly more real to us than all the strangeness of the Ituri Forest.

CANON MAURICE HEATH GARNER OF THE AFRICA INLAND MISSION

Father, help us to keep ourselves in your love wherever we are and whatever we are doing.

60. A Sure Defence

I will say of the Lord, He is my refuge. He shall cover thee with his feathers, and under his wings shalt thou trust. Thou shalt not be afraid for the terror by night; nor for the arrow that flieth by day *Psalm 91: 2, 4, 5*

One sunny morning in 1775 there was a visiting preacher at the meeting-house in Easton Township (New York State); and those were the words of his text. Silence followed his message, and then a Red Indian chief appeared at the open window, with a sheaf of poisoned arrows. None of the Friends moved.
With one noiseless bound, he stood at the doorway, and a dozen other Redskins ranged themselves beside their chief. In silence, the power of hate and the power of love were measured one against the other. At last the chief threw down his arrows and sat down; his followers, in their warpaint, did the same. The meeting went on, and a brooding Presence, in which the Indians seemed strangely at home, filled the room. At the close the patriarch of the Meeting invited the Indians by signs to his dwelling, and they accepted. There the chief said in broken English 'Indian come, see white man; no gun, no arrow; still; worshipping Great Spirit. Great Spirit inside Indian too, and say "Indian no kill". He took a white feather from an arrow, and made it firm over the centre of the roof. 'Indians your friends now.... you ours'—and henceforward they were.

VIOLET HODGKIN

O Lord, Thy promises are sure. Give us more of Thy Love and a greater trust in Thee.

SECTION THREE – Jesus Christ

61. Annunciation

The angel Gabriel was sent from God unto a city of Galilee, named Nazareth, to a virgin espoused to a man whose name was Joseph, of the house of David; and the virgin's name was Mary. And the angel said, Hail! thou that art highly favoured, the Lord is with thee: blessed art thou among women. Fear not, Mary: for thou hast found favour with God. And, behold, thou shalt conceive in thy womb, and bring forth a son, and shalt call his name Jesus. He shall be great, and shall be called the Son of the Highest: and of his kingdom there shall be no end. The Holy Ghost shall come upon thee. Therefore also that holy thing that shall be born of thee shall be called the Son of God. ...For with God nothing shall be impossible. And Mary said, Behold the handmaid of the Lord; be it unto me according to thy word.

Luke 1: 26–38 (selected)

What is the evidence for the Virgin Birth? The only possible evidence for any historical fact after so many years is that the men of that day, the only ones in a position to judge the evidence, believed it and put it forth as an authoritative statement about their Lord after the Resurrection. The very fact that St. Matthew and St. Luke wrote it down as their account of the Church's belief and that the Church accepted and put forth these Gospels as a true account of her belief, should be sufficient to show this. J. PATERSON SMYTH

O that Birth for ever blessed!
When the Virgin, full of grace,
By the Holy Ghost conceiving,
Bare the Saviour of our race. PRUDENTIUS

62. The Saviour Comes

And Mary brought forth her firstborn son, and wrapped him in swaddling clothes, and laid him in a manger; because there was no room for them in the inn. And there were in the same country shepherds abiding in the field, keeping watch over their flock by night. And, lo, the angel of the Lord came upon them, and the glory of the Lord shone around about them: and they were sore afraid. And the angel said unto them, Fear not: for, behold, I bring you good tidings of great joy, which shall be to all people. For unto you is born this day in the city of David a Saviour, which is Christ the Lord. And suddenly there was with the angel a multitude of the heavenly host praising God, and saying, Glory to God in the highest, and on earth peace, goodwill toward men. *Luke 2: 7–11, 13, 14*

"In the fulness of time, God sent his Son", and the first thing that strikes one is the simple, ordinary way in which the great thing happened. And yet, on second thoughts, is not this God's method in working all his wonders? That is how they do things in that Eternal World. In the building of an oak, in the making of a planet, in the wonder of the dawn, in the miracle of the yellow harvest—that seems God's method always; quiet, simple, unnoticed. J. PATERSON SMYTH

The great important message for today is the one the praising angels gave nearly two thousand years ago: Peace on earth—goodwill toward men.

O holy child of Bethlehem, descend to us, we pray;
Cast out our sin, and enter in; be-born in us today.
We hear the Christmas angels the great glad tidings tell;
O come to us, abide with us, Our Lord Immanuel.

PHILLIPS BROOKS

63. Word become Flesh

In the beginning was the Word, and the Word was with God, and the Word was God. The same was in the beginning with God. All things were made by him; and without him was not any thing made that was made. In him was life; and the life was the light of men. And the light shineth in darkness; and the darkness comprehended it not. *John 1: 1–5*

It is the most tremendous, the most incredible thing in the whole universe to believe. That God became Man. That the Word became Flesh. And as you think of the Christ-child in the dear old Christmas story, rest happy and peaceful in the simple old faith. Nothing has happened or can happen to disturb it. What the Church has been saying for two thousand years she will keep on saying till there are years no longer. "I believe in Jesus Christ, His only begotten Son our Lord, who was conceived by the Holy Ghost, born of the Virgin Mary".

J. Paterson Smyth

Yea, Lord, we greet Thee,
Born this happy morning;
Jesus, to Thee be glory given,
Word of the Father,
Now in flesh appearing:
O come, let us adore Him, Christ the Lord.

Anonymous
(17th or 18th cent.)

O perfect Love, outpassing sight,
O Light beyond our ken,
Come down through all the world tonight,
And heal the hearts of men.

Laurence Housman

64. Born in a Stable

And it came to pass as the angels were gone away from them into heaven, the shepherds said one to another. Let us now go unto Bethlehem and see this thing which has come to pass, which the Lord hath made known unto us. And they came with haste and found Mary and Joseph, and the babe lying in a manger. And when they had seen it, they made known abroad the saying which was told them concerning this child. And all they that heard it wondered at those things which were told them by the shepherds. But Mary kept all these things, and pondered them in her heart. *Luke 2: 15–19*

Did ever Baby enter this world in lowlier guise? And do we not all love Him the more for it? Somehow it would spoil the picture if He had been born in a palace with princesses to wait on Him and high priests in attendance...... Simply, ordinarily, as the coming of the dawn, happened this tremendous thing in the history of the universe, the coming of the Lord of Glory into human life. J. PATERSON SMYTH

To Bethlehem straight the enlightened shepherds ran,
To see the wonder God had wrought for man:
Then to their flocks, still praising God, return,
And their glad hearts with holy rapture burn;
Amazed, the wondrous tidings they proclaim,
The first apostles of His infant fame. JOHN BYROM

LORD GOD Almighty, Father of every family, against whom no door can be shut: Enter the homes of our land, we beseech thee, with the angel of thy presence, to hallow them in pureness and beauty of love; and by thy dear Son, born in a stable, move our hearts to hear the cry of the homeless, and to convert all sordid and bitter dwellings into households of thine; through Jesus Christ our Lord.

65. Jesus the Lord

And the shepherds returned, glorifying and praising God for all the things that they had heard and seen, as it was told unto them. And when eight days were accomplished for the circumcising of the child, his name was called JESUS, which was so named of the angel before he was conceived in the womb. *Luke 2: 20–21*

In the name of Jesus
Every knee shall bow,
Every tongue confess Him
King of Glory now;
'Tis the Father's pleasure
We should call Him Lord,
Who from the beginning
Was the mighty Word.

In your hearts enthrone Him;
There let Him subdue
All that is not holy,
All that is not true;
Crown Him as your Captain
In temptation's hour;
Let His will enfold you
In its light and power.

C. M. Noel

A new era began at the birth of Jesus. Before His birth —B.C. (Before Christ). Now it is Anno Domini (In the year of our Lord). From the point of view of Christian Faith there is nothing in time worthy to be set beside the deeds and the words of One who is adored as God manifest in the flesh, and the Saviour. W. P. Paterson

Come, divine and peaceful Guest, enter our devoted breast;
Life divine in us renew, Thou the Gift, and Giver too!

Charles Wesley

66. God's Moment

When the fulness of the time was come, God sent forth his Son. *Galatians 4: 4*

"In the fulness of time" God came to earth in Jesus Christ. When Christ came to earth, love came to earth. As they saw Him, men had the chance to know what God is like.

Only a human life could reveal God at all adequately, and even that could not reveal Him perfectly; but all that was possible appeared in Jesus. Love as revealed by Jesus wasn't sentimental, or indulgent, or concerned only with feeling... even his warnings and denunciations were the judgements of love. He was against whatever obscured the love of His Father, and it was love, also, for those who obscured it which made His warnings so sharp.

And He never gave up. When wickedness triumphed and hammered Him on the wood, love achieved a greater triumph. The wickedness couldn't hammer the love out of Him. W. E. SANGSTER

Eternal depth of love divine,
 In Jesus, God with us, displayed;
How bright Thy beaming glories shine!
 How wide Thy healing streams are spread!

NICOLAUS VON ZINZENDORF

Saviour, blessed Saviour,
Listen while we sing;
Hearts and voices raising
Praises to our King:

All we have we offer,
All we hope to be,
Body, soul, and spirit,
All we yield to Thee.

GODFREY THRING

67. The Enquiring Boy

Now it was the practice of his parents to go to Jerusalem every year for the Passover festival; and when he was twelve, they made the pilgrimage as usual. When the festive season was over, and they started for home, the boy Jesus stayed behind in Jerusalem. His parents returned to Jerusalem to look for him; and after three days they found him sitting in the temple surrounded by the teachers, listening to them and putting questions; and all who heard were amazed at his intelligence and the answers he gave. His mother said to him, 'My son... your father and I have been searching for you in great anxiety.' 'What made you search?' he said. 'Did you not know that I was bound to be in my Father's house?'

Luke 2: 41–49, NEB

It is as a Son that our Lord would have His disciples know Him. He uses the phrase 'my Father' thirty times, on nine occasions, so addressing God directly; and at least seventeen times He calls himself 'Son' or 'Son of God'... it denotes Him as holding to God a relation of unique intimacy and love. H. R. MACKINTOSH

I saw something that illuminated ... the story of Jesus disputing with the rabbis in the Temple. In one obscure synagogue in Jerusalem the morning service had just ended. A lad of about twelve years of age was standing before three bearded elders, talking to them in animated manner. Sometimes he pleased them ... but sometimes he annoyed them. But the little fellow stood his ground ... then, his questions over, he gave a little bob to the old men and walked away. H. V. MORTON

O Lord God, we do thank Thee for giving Thy Son Jesus Christ to the world. He has shown us that Thou art our *Father too, the universal Father who loves each one of His children, and that Thou art LOVE.*

68. The Baptist

John did baptize in the wilderness, and preach the baptism of repentance for the remission of sins... and preached, saying, There cometh one mightier than I after me, the latchet of whose shoes I am not worthy to stoop down and unloose. I indeed have baptized you with water: but he shall baptize you with the Holy Ghost. And it came to pass in those days, that Jesus came from Nazareth of Galilee, and was baptized of John in Jordan. And straightway coming up out of the water, he saw the heavens opened and the Spirit like a dove descending upon him: and there came a voice from heaven, saying, Thou art my beloved Son, in whom I am well pleased.

Mark 1: 4, 7–11

John the Baptist, whose mother was a kinswoman of the mother of Jesus, learnt the secret of spiritual strength as he communed with God in the solitude of the desert. Here the "Word of God" came to him... The baptism of John was the declaration unto all men that the condition of entrance into God's Kingdom is the putting away of sin. When Jesus was baptised of John, He did not come confessing sin—as did all the other men. The act marked His consecration to His Messanic work and His identification of Himself with sinners. John knew that his baptism was to prepare the way for the coming of a 'mightier' than he who would baptize with the Holy Spirit.

J. G. TASKER

In Palestine the dove was a sacred bird. It was not hunted and not eaten.

Spirit Divine, attend our prayers
And make our hearts Thy home;
Descend with all Thy gracious powers;
O come, great Spirit, come! ANDREW REED

69. Temptation

And Jesus being full of the Holy Ghost returned from Jordan, and was led by the Spirit into the wilderness, being forty days tempted of the devil.

Devil: If thou be the Son of God, command this stone that it be made bread.

Jesus: It is written that man shall not live by bread alone, but by every word of God.

The devil, taking him up into a high mountain, showed him all the kingdoms of the world in a moment of time.

Devil: All this power will I give thee, and the glory of them: for that is delivered unto me; and to whomsoever I will give it. If thou therefore wilt worship me, all shall be thine.

Jesus: Get thee behind me, Satan: for it is written, Thou shalt worship the Lord thy God, and him only shalt thou serve.

The devil brought him to Jerusalem, set him on a pinnacle of the temple.

Devil: If thou be the Son of God, cast thyself down from hence: for it is written, He shall give his angels charge over thee, to keep thee: and in their hands they shall bear thee up, lest at any time thou dash thy foot against a stone.

Jesus: It is said, Thou shalt not tempt the Lord thy God.

And Jesus returned in the power of the Spirit into Galilee. *Luke 4: 1–14 (adapted)*

This is the most sacred of stories, for it can have come from no other source than His own lips.

WILLIAM BARCLAY

Lord, we beseech Thee, give us strength to resist temptations.

70. Calling His Men

Jesus saw two ships standing by the lake—the fishermen were washing their nets. He entered one of the ships, which was Simon's, and he sat down and taught the people out of the ship. Now when he had left speaking, he said unto Simon, Launch out into the deep, and let down your nets for a draught. Simon said, Master, we have toiled all the night and have taken nothing: nevertheless at thy word I will let down the net. And when they had this done, they enclosed a great multitude of fishes: and their net brake. And they beckoned unto their partners and they came, and filled both the ships, so that they began to sink... And when they had brought their ships to land, they forsook all, and followed him. *Luke 5: 1–11 (selected)*

How tired, depressed, and hungry Simon and his partners must have been. The words of Jesus must surely have annoyed them. How silly! Simon probably thought. But he obeyed—then came the miracle. I love this story—it is in line with the feeding of the five thousand from five loaves and two fishes. Let us obey our Master when he tells us to 'launch out'.

As, of old, apostles heard it
By the Galilean lake
Turned from home and toil and kindred,
Leaving all for His dear sake.

Jesus calls us! By Thy mercies,
Saviour, make us hear Thy call,
Give our hearts to Thine obedience,
Serve and love Thee best of all.

C. F. ALEXANDER

71. Caring for Daily Needs

When Jesus lifted up his eyes, and saw a great company come unto him, he saith unto Philip, Whence shall we buy bread, that these may eat? Philip answered, Two hundred pennyworth of bread is not sufficient for them. Andrew saith unto him, There is a lad here, which hath five barley loaves, and two small fishes: but what are they among so many? Jesus said, Make the men sit down. So the men sat down, in number about five thousand. And Jesus took the loaves; and when he had given thanks, he distributed to the disciples, and the disciples to them that were set down, and likewise of the fishes as much as they could. *John 6: 5–11*

The boy was there with his lunch when Jesus needed him. Just so have thousands upon thousands of ordinary men and women been near at hand for Christ's use ever since.

We, like the disciples, may be helpless as we face a situation too big for our resources. Yet the little we have may be enough if Christ is allowed to use it.

International Bible Reading Association Daily Notes

Our job as "followers" is to share and care—to follow our Master's example. Sharing, and caring, with love in our hearts. Love is a Helping Hand.

Almighty God, we give Thee thanks for feeding and renewing us; We offer Thee ourselves, our souls, bodies, to be a living sacrifice, through Jesus Christ our Lord. Send us out into the world in the power of Thy spirit, to love and work to Thy praise and glory.

(Words said together after Communion at St. George's Cathedral, Jerusalem, on St. George's Day 1972)

72. Transfiguration

And Jesus said unto them (the disciples), But whom say ye that I am? Peter said, The Christ of God. And it came to pass about an eight days after these sayings, he took Peter and John and James, and went up into a mountain to pray. And as he prayed, the fashion of his countenance was altered, and his raiment was white and glistering. And, behold, there talked with him two men, which were Moses and Elias: who appeared in glory, and spake of his decease which he should accomplish at Jerusalem.

And there came a voice out of the cloud, This is my beloved Son: hear him. *Luke 9: 20, 28–31, 35*

The glory is not reflected light; its source is inward. It is the manifestation of a mental process.
The Voice stood for the acceptance of His work by God. He was enabled to yield up His heart and life anew to the will of God. The great lesson for His disciples was that the dreadful shame of His cross was really glory and that all suffering is ultimately radiant with heavenly beauty being perfected in Christ.

R. H. STRACHAN

It is good to be with Him whose last best word is Love.

(ADAPTED FROM A HYMN BY A. P. STANLEY)

Jesus, these eyes have never seen
That radiant form of Thine;
The veil of sense hangs dark between
Thy blessed face and mine.

Yet though I have not seen, and still
Must rest in faith alone;
I love Thee, dearest Lord, and will,
Unseen but not unknown.

RAY PALMER

73. The Way the Master Went

And it came to pass, when the time was come that he should be received up, he stedfastly set his face to go to Jerusalem. *Luke 9: 51*

This is one of the most poignant sentences in the New Testament. Jesus—strong, vigorous, only thirty-three years old ... healing the sick, making the blind to see and the deaf to hear. Such a few years He has had to serve His heavenly Father, and do His will. Why should He die? Why should He suffer a terrible death when never had He done anything wrong... only healed and blessed and done His Father's will? What would His friends do without Him? Who would carry on His work? But in the same chapter we read of His being alone praying (v. 18), and then of His Transfiguration, when again the voice of God came, "This is my beloved Son". And the Son must gladly obey the will of the Father, even to the Cross, for He knew that was what awaited Him. How Jesus trusted God!... but, being man, what a struggle He must have had with His own wishes.
Praise God, Hallelujah, His Son obeyed—and we, His children and the whole world are reaping the benefit. For the Son showed the Way to God, Peace and Love.

Forward! be our watchword, steps and voices joined; seek the things before us, not a look behind... Who shall dream of shrinking, by our Captain led?

HENRY ALFORD

Guide me, O Thou great Jehovah,
Pilgrim through this barren land;
I am weak, but Thou art mighty;
Hold me with Thy powerful hand:
Bread of heaven!
Feed me now and evermore. W. WILLIAMS

74. Jesus and the Individual

And Jesus entered and passed through Jericho. And, behold, there was a man named Zacchaeus, which was the chief among the publicans, and he was rich. And he sought to see Jesus who he was; and climbed up into a sycomore tree to see him; for he was to pass that way. And when Jesus came to the place, he looked up, and saw him, and said unto him, Zacchaeus, make haste, and come down; for today I must abide at thy house. And he made haste, and came down, and received him joyfully. And when they saw it, they all murmured, saying, That he was gone to be guest with a man that is a sinner. Jesus said unto Zacchaeus, The Son of man is come to seek and to save that which was lost.

Luke 19: 1–7, 10

Even when Jesus is surrounded by a crowd He always sees people singly and not in the mass. The gospels are full of stories of Jesus singling out individuals even when the crowds thronged Him. In all cases they were healed in mind as well as body, or as in the case of the Samaritan woman and Zacchaeus they found that their deepest needs were met.

Note that Jesus saw Zacchaeus not as he was in the sight of his fellows but as he could become. His belief was vindicated when Zacchaeus made a voluntary renunciation of half his possessions and the vow to restore fourfold what he had wrongly extorted. In like fashion even in our shortcomings He never sees us as we are but as what we have the power to be. When Jesus deals with us we are under no delusions about our past but we have a new confidence in our future.

International Bible Reading Association Daily Notes

We thank Thee, Father, for Thy belief in what we may become, and we pray Thee help us to fulfil Thy plan for us.

75. Jesus the King

Jesus sent two of his disciples, saying, Go ye into the village; ye shall find a colt tied: loose him, and bring him hither. If any man ask you, Why do ye loose him? say, Because the Lord hath need of him. And they brought him to Jesus: and set Jesus thereon. As he went, they spread their clothes in the way. And when he was come nigh, at the descent of the mount of Olives, the whole multitude of the disciples began to rejoice and praise God saying, Blessed be the King that cometh in the name of the Lord: peace in heaven, and glory in the highest. *Luke 19: 29, 30, 35–38 (selected)*

It was carefully planned. THE LORD NEEDS IT was a password chosen long ago. It was an act of glorious defiance. It is impossible to exaggerate the sheer courage of Jesus. It was a deliberate claim to be a King. The ass in Palestine was not the lowly beast that it is in this country. Only in war did kings ride upon a horse; when they came in peace they came upon an ass. So Jesus by this action came as the king who comes to His people in love and in peace.

WILLIAM BARCLAY

Hark the glad sound! the Saviour comes,
The Saviour promised long;
Let every heart prepare a throne,
And every voice a song.

PHILIP DODDRIDGE

Thou didst accept their praises; Accept the prayers we bring,
Who in all good delightest, Thou good and gracious King.

THEODULF OF ORLEANS

76. Righteous Anger

Mine house shall be called an house of prayer for all people. *Isaiah 56: 7*

And they come to Jerusalem: and Jesus went into the temple, and began to cast out them that sold and bought in the temple, and overthrew the tables of the money-changers, and the seats of them that sold doves; and would not suffer that any man should carry any vessel through the temple. And he taught, saying unto them, Is it not written, My house shall be called of all nations the house of prayer? but ye have made it a den of thieves. And the scribes and chief priests heard it, and sought how they might destroy him. *Mark 11: 15–18*

In this passage we see the anger of Jesus that is opposed to all that keeps men from God. He turns out of the temple all those who had turned it into a place of commerce and profit.

On the rock of Edinburgh Castle there is built a small chapel in memory of St. Margaret of Scotland. For many years its windows were bricked in, its door was padlocked, and it was used as an arsenal, men forgetting with the years that it had been built as a house of God. In the last century a visitor was looking at the small, neglected building and realized that it was an ancient chapel. Through his perception it was restored to its former beauty and used again as a place of prayer.

International Bible Reading Association Daily Notes

Strong in the Lord of Hosts, and in His mighty power,
Who in the strength of Jesus trusts is more than
conqueror. CHARLES WESLEY

Lord, when I see something that I know is wrong, give me strength and courage to do something about it.

77. The Last Supper

Now the feast of unleavened bread drew nigh, which is called the Passover. And the chief priests and scribes sought how they might kill Jesus; for they feared the people. Then entered Satan into Judas surnamed Iscariot, being of the number of the twelve. And he went his way, and communed with the chief priests and captains, how he might betray him unto them. *Luke 22: 1–6*

What Judas betrayed to the authorities was probably where Jesus could be found. Why he did it is not so certain. Perhaps in delivering Jesus into the hands of His enemies, Judas was trying to force Him to manifest His powers. This could explain his final remorse. The action of Jesus was deeply symbolic. They were to eat and drink in remembrance of God's great act of redemption in the past. When Jesus gives His disciples His body and His blood, He gives Himself to them in order that they may be partakers of His sacrifice. The fruit of the sacrifice once offered by Christ is an ever abiding food and drink, a spring of strength and joy to His Church.

Bible Reading Fellowship notes

Jesus, to Thy table led,
Now let every heart be fed
With the true and living Bread.

R. H. BAYNES

In the Lord's Supper we have a foretaste of a redeemed society when all men can live as brothers in peace and goodness, a pledge that one day Christ will come again.

Be known to us in breaking bread,
But do not then depart;
Saviour, abide with us, and spread
Thy table in our heart. J. MONTGOMERY

78. The World's Light

Then spake Jesus again unto them, saying, I am the light of the world: he that followeth me shall not walk in darkness but shall have the light of life. I am the way, and the truth, and the life. No man cometh unto the Father but by me. *John 8: 12; John 14: 6*

I heard the voice of Jesus say;
I am this dark world's Light;
Look unto Me, thy morn shall rise,
And all thy day be bright.
I looked to Jesus, and I found
In Him my star, my sun,
And in that light of life I'll walk
Till travelling days are done.

HORATIUS BONAR

Those who follow Jesus in faith shall be led from the darkness of sin and death, into the Light of Life.
"Follow thou Me" is, in a very real sense, the sum of all Christian duty.

The Promise Book

Thou art the Way: to Thee alone
From sin and death we flee:
Thou art the Truth: Thy word alone
True wisdom can impart;
Thou art the Life: the rending tomb
Proclaims Thy conquering arm;
Thou art the Way, the Truth, the Life:
Grant us that Way to know,

GEORGE W. DOANE

79. Do this...

And Jesus took bread, and gave thanks, and brake it, and gave unto them, saying, This is my body, which is given for you: this do in remembrance of me. Likewise also the cup after supper, saying, This cup is the new testament in my blood, which is shed for you.

Luke 22: 19, 20

The Lord's Supper has continued throughout the centuries from the days of the earliest Church down to the present day. What does it mean to us?
IT IS A THANKSGIVING. Thanks to God for His great goodness to us—most of all for the gift of Jesus Christ.
IT IS A MEMORIAL. A perpetual commemoration of Christ's sacrificial death.
IT IS A COMMUNION. Through this rite we can experience real fellowship with our Lord... In our normal occupations, in the reading of His word.
IT IS A SACRAMENT. (*Sacramentum,* a soldier's oath of allegiance). It is a renewal of the Christian soldier's promise of allegiance to his Master and his Lord.
IT HAS A SOCIAL SIGNIFICANCE. All those who are Christ's enter into fellowship with one another as well as with their Lord. SOURCE UNKNOWN

In memory of the Saviour's love
  We keep the sacred feast,
Where every humble, contrite heart
  Is made a welcome guest.

THOMAS COTTERILL

Holy Lord, O come in this sweet hour, feed me with food divine; and fill with all Thy love and power this worthless heart of mine. HENRY W. BAKER

80. Humility

And supper being ended Jesus laid aside his garments; and took a towel, and girded himself. After that he poureth water into a bason, and began to wash the disciples' feet, and to wipe them with the towel wherewith he was girded. The cometh he to Simon Peter; and Peter saith unto him, Lord, dost thou wash my feet? Jesus answered and said unto him, What I do thou knowest not now; but thou shalt know hereafter. Peter saith unto him, Thou shalt never wash my feet. Jesus answered, If I wash thee not, thou hast no part with me. Simon Peter saith unto him, Lord, not my feet only, but also my hands and my head. *John 13: 2–9*

They had put off their sandals as they entered the room, and reclined with hot, tired, dusty feet—no one there to do the foot-washing, except the Lord of the Universe, who had so often taught them that the greatest is he that serves. Startled, self-reproachful, they kept silent till he came to Peter. "Thou shalt never wash my feet, Lord,"—then, with his usual impulsiveness, "not my feet only!"... So Jesus went the round. Think of him washing the feet of Judas! and the secret horror of the man who knew where those feet had taken him the previous night! Then, when He had resumed His place, He uttered His quiet rebuke. J. PATERSON SMYTH

Just at that moment when He might have had the supreme pride, He had the supreme himility. Love is always like that. When, for example, someone falls ill, the person who loves him will perform the most menial services and will delight to do them, because love is like that. WILLIAM BARCLAY

O God, teach us the lesson of humility. May we wait on others without thought of self.

81. The Vine and the Branches

I am the true vine, and my Father is the husbandman. Abide in me, and I in you. As the branch cannot bear fruit of itself, except it abide in the vine; no more can ye, except ye abide in me. I am the vine, ye are the branches: he that abideth in me, and I in him, the same bringeth forth much fruit: for without me ye can do nothing. If ye abide in me, and my words abide in you, ye shall ask what ye will, and it shall be done unto you. Herein is my Father glorified, that ye bear much fruit; so shall ye be my disciples. As the Father hath loved me, so have I loved you: continue ye in my love.

John 15: 1, 4, 5, 7–9

This last 'I AM' links Jesus with us in the closest possible bond. Branches can have no existence apart from the tree... Just as truly as branches are nourished by the sap that flows into them, so our souls are fed by the life of Christ. On the other hand, there is a sense in which Christ needs us too. The vine vitalizes its branches so that they may yield healthy fruit. We are Christ's emissaries to BEAR MUCH FRUIT for him in the world. *Bible Reading Fellowship notes*

If we are united to Jesus Christ, as the branches of a vine are united to the main stock, we should show the fruit of the Spirit—'love, joy, peace, patience, kindness, goodness, faithfulness, gentleness, self-control' in our Christian witness.

International Bible Reading Association notes

It passeth telling, that dear love of Thine,
My Saviour, Jesus! Yet these lips of mine
Would fain proclaim to sinners far and near
A love which can remove all guilty fear, and love beget.

MARY SHEKLETON

82. The Bitter Cup

And Jesus came out, and went, as he was wont, to the Mount of Olives; and his disciples followed him. And when he was at the place, he said unto them, Pray that ye enter not into temptation. And he was withdrawn from them about a stone's cast, and kneeled down, and prayed. *Luke 22: 39–41*

Father, if it be possible, let this cup pass from me: nevertheless not as I will, but as thou wilt.
Matthew 26: 39

What a bitter cup for Jesus, yet what a blessing for the whole wide world that Jesus obeyed God's will—that He allowed hate to do its worst. And Love conquered death. Now Christ is the Saviour of the world. He has shown us that Love is the greatest thing in the world and the only thing to save the world from destruction. Sacrifice and Love go together. The whole world, everyone in it, has been enriched by the sacrifice of Jesus on the Cross, and by coming to Him we are enriched, body, soul and mind.

Into the woods my Master went,
Clean forspent, forspent;
Into the woods my Master came,
Forspent with love and shame.

Out of the woods my Master went,
And he was well content,
Out of the woods my Master came,
Content with death and shame.

SIDNEY LANIER

May we, O loving Father, put our complete trust in Thee, and face life to come without fear, knowing that we are in Thy keeping.

83. Pilate

When the morning was come and when they had bound him, they led him away, and delivered him to Pontius Pilate the governor. Now at that feast the governor was wont to release unto the people a prisoner, whom they would. Therefore when they were gathered together, Pilate said unto them, Whom will ye that I release unto you? Barabbas, or Jesus which is called Christ? For he knew that for envy they had delivered him. The chief priests and elders persuaded the multitude that they should ask Barabbas, and destroy Jesus. Then released he Barabbas unto them: and when he had scourged Jesus, he delivered him to be crucified.

Matthew 27: 1, 2, 15, 17, 20, 26 (selected)

Pilate tried to take the weak man's way out, and evade the responsibility. No such evasion was possible—it was still Pilate's act. Hence in the subsequent life of the Christian Church it is the name of the weak Pilate instead of the treacherous Judas, or the scheming Caiaphas, which has become indissolubly linked with the crucifixion of Jesus. He 'suffered under Pontius Pilate'. *Source unknown*

My song is love unknown;
My Saviour's love to me;
Love to the loveless shown,
That they may lovely be.

O who am I,
That for my sake,
My Lord should take
Frail flesh and die?

SAMUEL CROSSMAN

Thou camest, O Lord, with the living word that should set Thy people free;
But, with mocking scorn and with crown of thorn,
They bore Thee to Calvary;
O come to my heart, Lord Jesus;
Thy Cross is my only plea. EMILY E. S. ELLIOTT

84. Calvary

And when they were come to the place called Calvary, there they crucified him, and the malefactors, one on the right hand, and the other on the left. Then said Jesus, Father, forgive them; for they know not what they do....
And the malefactor said unto Jesus, Lord, remember me when thou comest into thy kingdom. And Jesus said unto him, Verily I say unto thee, Today shalt thou be with me in paradise. *Luke 23: 33, 34, 42, 43*

Think of the generous heart of that dying Jesus, who could actually try to find an excuse—not merely forgive—not merely pray for—but actually try to find something in their favour. One at least heard. "There were two malefactors crucified with Jesus". Now one is growing silent... he is ashamed of himself... And then—it happened. Father, forgive! And lo! a miracle. In an instant the man is changed, suddenly converted! So came to that poor robber forgiveness and peace, and a promise of life at the other side of death. If anyone knew, Jesus knew. J. PATERSON SMYTH

Undismayed, His foes forgiving, to the last for others living,
Lays He down His life for all; love heroic, love unshrinking,
Heaven and earth together linking, reigns he, as the shadows fall.

A. F.

Therefore kind Jesu, since I cannot pay Thee,
I do adore Thee, and will ever pray Thee,
Think on Thy pity and Thy love unswerving,
Not my deserving.

JOHANN HEERMANN

85. He died for Me

And they crucified him . . . and set up over his head his accusation written, THIS IS JESUS THE KING OF THE JEWS. Now from the sixth hour there was darkness over all the land until the ninth hour. And many women were there beholding afar off, which followed Jesus from Galilee, ministering unto him.

Matthew 27: 35, 37, 45, 55, 57

The facts of the Cross are too horrifying to be told in any detail—nailed with fierce rough nails—hung in intense heat with unbearable thirst, exposed to the mockery of the crowds. If ever cruel punishment could be devised for the very worst of criminals, it was this lingering, agonising death by crucifixion.

DAVID C. K. WATSON

When I survey the wondrous Cross
On which the Prince of Glory died,
My richest gain I count but loss
And pour contempt on all my pride.

Were the whole realm of nature mine,
That were an offering far too small;
Love so amazing, so divine,
Demands my soul, my life, my all.

ISAAC WATTS

Almighty and everlasting God, who, of Thy tender love towards mankind, hast sent Thy Son, our Saviour Jesus Christ, to take upon Him our flesh, and to suffer death upon the cross, that all mankind should follow the example of His great humility; mercifully grant, that we may both follow the example of His patience, and also be made partakers of His resurrection.

Collect for the Sunday before Easter.
(Book of Common Prayer)

86. The Empty Tomb

Now upon the first day of the week, very early in the morning, they came unto the sepulchre, bringing the spices which they had prepared, and certain others with them. And they found the stone rolled away from the sepulchre. And they entered in, and found not the body of the Lord Jesus. And it came to pass, as they were much perplexed thereabout, behold, two men stood by in shining garments: and as they were afraid, and bowed down their faces to the earth, they said unto them, Why seek ye the living among the dead? He is not here, but is risen. *Luke 24: 1–6*

One thing is certain, if Jesus had not risen from the dead we would never have heard of Him. The attitude of the women was that they had come to pay the last tribute to a dead body. The attitude of the disciples was that everything had finished in tragedy. Nothing else could have changed sad and despairing men and women into people radiant with joy and flaming with courage. The Resurrection is the central fact of the whole Christian faith. WILLIAM BARCLAY

I have heard people say: Isn't life futile? Indeed it is, if we don't believe that this was one grave that gave back its Occupant, and that One was Jesus, the Son of God. By rising from the dead He revealed to the whole world that death was not the final arbiter of our destiny, because life was stronger than death and love larger than life. CANON CLIFFORD-PRONGER

Thine be the glory, risen, conquering Son,
Endless is the victory Thou o'er death hast won.
No more we doubt Thee, glorious Prince of life;
Life is nought without Thee: aid us in the strife.

E. L. BUDRY

87. The Road to Emmaus

And, behold, two of them went that same day to a village called Emmaus... and they talked together of all these things which had happened. While they communed together and reasoned, Jesus himself drew near, and went with them. But their eyes were holden that they should not know him. And he said unto them, What manner of communications are these that ye have one to another, as ye walk, and are sad? And one of them; Cleopas, answering said unto him, Art thou only a stranger in Jerusalem, and hast not known the things which are come to pass there in these days... concerning Jesus of Nazareth?... Then he expounded unto them... the scriptures... concerning himself. And it came to pass, as he sat at meat with them, he took bread, and blessed it, and brake, and gave to them. And their eyes were opened, and they knew him.

Luke 24: 13–19, 27, 30, 31

'Yea, I know!' cried the true man of old: 'and whoso'er wills it may know, "My Redeemer — He liveth!" I seek for a sign of His presence, and lo, as He spake to the light, and it was, so He speaks to my soul and I know!'

SOLOMON SOLIS-COHEN

The living Lord came to the disciples in several ways on the first Easter Day: at the tomb; on the road to Emmaus; in the upper room. When Jesus came there was amazement at first, but when the disciples realized that things were happening just as He had told them, everything was changed.

Thy Word is a Lamp (I.B.R.A.)

Lord Jesus, in the days of old two walked with Thee in waning light. As night descends, we too would pray: O leave us not at close of day! JAMES A. NOBLE

88. Alive for Evermore

And after eight days again his disciples were within, and Thomas with them. Then came Jesus, the doors being shut, and stood in the midst, and said, Peace be unto you. Then saith he to Thomas, Reach hither thy hand, and thrust it into my side: and be not faithless, but believing. And Thomas answered and said unto him, My Lord and my God. Jesus saith unto him, Thomas, because thou hast seen me, thou hast believed: blessed are they that have not seen, and yet have believed.

John 20: 26–28

Thomas, when he was sure, went the whole way: "My Lord and my God!" Thomas doubted to become sure, and when he did become sure his surrender to certainty was complete.

This was the message that absolutely thrilled those first Christians: God had given them overwhelming proof that Jesus Christ was what He claimed to be. God had set His final seal by raising Him from the dead. They knew it to be true. DAVID C. K. WATSON

We need to remember that Christianity is not founded just on Jesus the good man who died a martyr's death, but on the risen Christ.

International Bible Reading Association Daily Notes.

Friend of mine, friend divine, He will leave me never,
Died for me, set me free, now He lives for ever.
Loves and guides from day to day, He is ever near me,
Saviour mine, Christ divine, when I call will hear me.
Friend of mine, Christ divine, be my Saviour ever.

Source unknown

89. Risen Lord

And as they thus spake, Jesus himself stood in the midst of them, and saith unto them, Peace be unto you. And they were terrified and affrighted, and supposed that they had seen a spirit. And he said unto them, Why are ye troubled? and why do thoughts arise in your hearts? Behold my hands and my feet, that it is I myself: handle me, and see; for a spirit hath not flesh and bones, as ye see me have. And when he had thus spoken, he showed them his hands and his feet. And while they yet believed not for joy, and wondered, he said unto them, Have ye here any meat? And they gave him a piece of broiled fish, and an honeycomb. And he took it, and did eat before them. *Luke 24: 36–43*

Death cannot keep his prey,
Jesus, my Saviour;
He tore the bars away,
Jesus, my Lord.

ROBERT LOWRY

Christ is risen! The Resurrection faith will save us from the desolate unbelief which thinks that all the messages of the living Christ have been spoken to the dead, and that for us there is no word. He speaks, not to contradict any word that proceeded from His mouth, but to enlarge, to interpret, reconcile. He still leads the generations on.

W. ROBERTSON NICOLL

Make us quiet enough to listen, humble enough to understand, pure-hearted enough to see Him, until we know *that He is here with us, whom death could not hold, with us our Master and Friend and King for ever.*

LESLIE D. WEATHERHEAD

90. The Disciples' Joy

And Jesus said unto them, It behoved Christ to suffer, and that repentance and remission of sins should be preached in his name. And, behold, I send the promise of my Father upon you: but tarry ye in the city of Jerusalem, until ye be endued with power from on high. And he lifted up his hands and blessed them. And they returned with great joy.

Luke 24: 44, 46, 47, 49, 50, 52

Those last words impel me to believe that Christ surely rose from the dead. When a loved one leaves us for good, do we dance with joy and continually praise and thank God? Yes! I have been to a Quaker funeral when my black hat was the only sign of mourning... but the dead Friend was over eighty and we praised his good life. Christ was only thirty-three and he had died a criminal's death. They were going back to their old occupations depressed and sad. All their hopes were dashed to the ground and they must have been afraid of returning to where he had been taken prisoner. But now—they were full of joy and gladness and returned to Jerusalem, and in the Temple praised God (where His enemies were), all fear had gone. Their faces shone with joy.

Up from the grave He arose,
With a mighty triumph o'er His foes;
He arose a Victor from the dark domain,
And He lives for ever with His saints to reign:
He arose! Hallelujah! Christ arose!

ROBERT LOWRY

Dear Lord, our hearts, like your disciples', will be full of faith and love, for Thou art with us now, helping, guiding forgiving and LOVING us. May we ever follow Thee in love and peace—and joy.

SECTIOM FOUR – The Holy Spirit

91. Creative Spirit

In the beginning God created the heaven and the earth. And the earth was without form, and void; and darkness was upon the face of the deep. And the Spirit of God moved upon the face of the waters. *Genesis 1: 1, 2*

The Spirit of God hath made me, and the breath of the Almighty hath given me life. *Job 33: 4*

We meet the Spirit of God in the first words of the Bible. It is the Spirit of God who brings existence out of nothingness, order out of chaos, beauty out of blank formlessness. What is it that maintains the order of the heavens? . . . that makes this a reliable universe in which we can have faith? The answer of the Old Testament thinker would be that the Spirit of God brought order into chaos, and maintains the order of the world. If we wish to see the work of the Spirit, we have no further to look than the wonderful world. WILLIAM BARCLAY

Creator Spirit; by whose aid
The world's foundations first were laid;
Come, visit every waiting mind,
Come, pour Thy joys on human kind;
From sin and sorrow set us free,
And make Thy temples worthy Thee.
ANON. TR. JOHN DRYDEN

O Lord, how manifold are thy works! In wisdom hath thou made them all: the earth is full of thy riches. Thou sendest forth thy spirit, they are created: and thou renewest the face of the earth. Psalm 104: 24, 30

92. The Spirit in the Old Testament

And the Spirit of God moved upon the face of the waters. And God said, Let there be light: and there was light.

Genesis 1: 2, 3

By the word of the Lord were the heavens made; and all the host of them by the breath of his mouth.

Psalm 33: 6

The Spirit in the Old Testament. The conception of the "Spirit of God" is characteristic, being closely related to the Word. The distinction between them is that between the breath, and the voice—the latter being the articulate expression of thought, and the former the force by which the Word is made living. The Spirit is the life of God, and as such, is life-giving. The account of the creation in Genesis puts us in possession of the root idea. It was no blind force inherent in nature which produced the beautiful world, but a divine Thinker.
The Spirit is the life of God communicated by 'Word'. This creative principle, which animates the universe, finds a special sphere of activity in man, who by its operation becomes not only a living soul, but a rational being created in the image of God and reproducing the Divine life.

J. G. SIMPSON

Greater than stars that swim in space,
More real than time or tide,
Is God's unseen compelling grace
Man's boundless thought to guide.

B. R.

Breathe on me, Breath of God;
Fill me with life anew,
That I may love what Thou dost love
And do what Thou wouldst do.

EDWIN HATCH

93. The Spirit Within

A new heart also will I give you, and a new spirit will I put within you: and I will give you an heart of flesh. And I will put my spirit within you, and cause you to walk in my statutes, and ye shall keep my judgments and do them. *Ezekiel 36: 26, 27*

The Spirit of God is synonymous with the divine energy. The Spirit is active in creation, is the source of intellect in man and of special endowments and is the inspirer of lawgivers, poets, and prophets.

Holy Spirit, power Divine,
Fill and nerve this will of mine,
By Thee may I strongly live,
Bravely bear, and nobly strive.

Holy Spirit, peace Divine,
Still this restless heart of mine,
Speak to calm this tossing sea,
Stayed in Thy tranquility.

Holy Spirit, joy Divine,
Gladden Thou this heart of mine;
In the desert ways I'll sing:
Spring, O Well, for ever spring!

SAMUEL LONGFELLOW

Give me, O Lord, a steadfast heart, which no unworthy affection may drag downwards; give me an unconquered heart, which no tribulation can wear out; give me an upright heart, which no unworthy purpose may tempt aside. Bestow upon me also, O Lord my God, understanding to know Thee, diligence to seek Thee, and wisdom to find Thee. ST. THOMAS AQUINAS

94. The Spirit and John the Baptist

I indeed baptise you with water but one mighter than I cometh, the latchet of whose shoes I am unworthy to unloose: he shall baptise you with the Holy Ghost and with fire. *Luke 3: 16*

And John bare record, saying, I saw the Spirit descending from heaven like a dove, and it abode upon him. The same is he which baptizeth with the Holy Ghost. And I saw and bare record that this is the Son of God. *John 1: 32–34*

John the Baptist's great significance is not that he baptised, but that he pointed people to Jesus; what he knew by prophetic insight he shared with the people of his day. How concerned are we in this twentieth century to be signposts to Christ among our fellows? As Christians we have personal experience of Jesus, we know what he has done for us, and we have accounts of his life and teaching in four Gospels. Are we doing anything specific to represent him in the world?

International Bible Reading Association Daily Notes

To the Jew there were always three basic ideas of the Spirit... The Spirit was power, like a rushing mighty wind. The Spirit was the very centre and essence of life; The Spirit was God; the power and the life of the Spirit were beyond mere human achievement and attainment.

WILLIAM BARCLAY

Come, Holy Spirit, heavenly Dove,
With all Thy quickening powers;
Kindle a flame of sacred love
In these cold hearts of ours.

ISAAC WATTS

95. The Spirit in Jesus

And Jesus returned in the power of the Spirit into Galilee... And he came to Nazareth where he had been brought up: and as his custom was, he went into the synagogue on the sabbath day and stood up to read. And there was delivered unto him the book of the prophet Esaias. And when he opened the book, he found the place where it was written, The Spirit of the Lord is upon me, because he hath anointed me to preach the Gospel to the poor: he hath sent me to heal the broken-hearted, to preach deliverance to the captives, and recovering of sight to the blind, to set at liberty them that are bruised, to preach the acceptable year of the Lord. And he closed the book, and gave it again to the minister and sat down. And the eyes of all them that were in the synagogue were fastened on him.

Luke 4: 16–20

The main task of Jesus on earth was to reveal the Father, to disclose the true nature of the Kingdom of God and... to attach a few faithful souls to Himself as the foundation of His new kingdom, and for the after duty of spreading the gospel among mankind.

We see Jesus, in the power of the Holy Spirit, at the commencement of His ministry publicly identifying Himself with the One who had been prophesied would come. *Dictionary of the Bible;* JAMES HASTINGS

Come Holy Ghost, our hearts inspire, let us Thine influence prove,
Source of the old prophetic fire, fountain of light and love. CHARLES WESLEY

O Lord, give me Thy loving Spirit, I beseech Thee, so that I, too, may do Thy will and serve Thee aright.

96. The Promised Comforter

The Comforter, which is the Holy Ghost, whom the Father will send in my name, he shall teach you all things, and bring all things to your remembrance, whatsoever I have said unto you. *John 14: 26*

Pentecost adds nothing to the equipment of doctrines: it adds everything to the equipment of the teachers. What then is the real increment? The right way to understand the difference which the great visitation made is to imagine what would have happened if they had gone on without it, if they had not tarried in Jerusalem for the Divine equipment. They might have made some progress. In that case Peter might have said to the first believers, "We are now a hundred and twenty in number, and Christ is risen; perhaps by the end of the year we shall be a hundred and twenty-one". But what saith the Scripture? "The same day there were added to the church three thousand souls" (Acts 2. 4). That was the difference; they could see the mustard-seed grow and become a tree as they watched it. What is necessary is that we should hunger and thirst after righteousness. What is certain is that if we do so hunger we shall be sated (gratified to the full). F. RENDELL HARRIS

Is it outstanding personalities that build up a work of God, or is it the Holy Spirit working through surrendered lives? C.T. (Studd) and his wife were never in any doubt about it. They knew and declared their own nothingness, and that all that had been done was the work of the Spirit of God, which He will do through anyone who will utterly believe and obey Him.

N. P. GRUBB

Jesus, we on the word depend, spoken by Thee while present here: The Father in My name shall send the Holy Ghost, the Comforter. CHARLES WESLEY

97. Spirit of Power

And as they thus spake, Jesus himself stood in the midst of them. Then opened he their understanding, that they might understand the Scriptures, and said unto them, Thus it is written, and thus it behoved Christ to suffer, and to rise from the dead the third day: and that repentance and remission of sins should be preached in his name among all nations, beginning at Jerusalem. And ye are witnesses of these things. And, behold, I send the promise of my Father upon you: but tarry ye in the city of Jerusalem, until ye be endued with power from on high. *Luke 24: 36, 45–49*

1. This passage stresses the *Reality of the Resurrection.* He was real. The Jesus who died was in truth the Christ who rose agin. Christianity is not founded on the dreams of men's disordered minds, or the visions of their fevered eyes, but on one who in actual historical fact faced and fought and conquered death and rose again.

2. It stresses the *Necessity of the Cross*... It was part of the plan of God, for the Cross is the one place on earth where, in a moment of time, we see the eternal love of God.

3. It stresses the *Urgency of the Task.* Out to all men had to go the call to repentance and the offer of forgiveness.

4. It stresses the *Secret of Power.* They had to wait in Jerusalem until power from on high came upon them, until Pentecost had come. There is a time to wait on God and a time to work for God.

WILLIAM BARCLAY

98. Not you, but the Spirit

But take heed to yourselves; for they shall deliver you to the councils... But when they shall lead you and deliver you up, take no thought beforehand what ye shall speak, neither do ye premeditate; but whatsoever shall be given you in that hour, that speak ye: for it is not ye that speak, but the Holy Ghost... he that shall endure to the end, the same shall be saved.

Mark 13: 9, 11, 13

In all the Synoptic Gospels—Matthew, Mark, Luke—we have the assurance from Jesus: we too shall be given the words to say on God's behalf, when called upon.

The Master calls! Arise and go; how blest His messenger to be! He, who hath given thee liberty, now bids thee set the captives free.

E. MAY GRIMES

Gracious Spirit, Holy Ghost,
Taught by Thee we covet most
Of Thy gifts at Pentecost
Holy, Heavenly Love.

Love is kind, and suffers long;
Love is meek, and thinks no wrong;
Love than death itself more strong;
Therefore give us Love.

CHRISTOPHER WORDSWORTH

99. Ever-present Spirit

Go ye therefore, and teach all nations, baptizing them in the name of the Father, and of the Son, and of the Holy Ghost; teaching them to observe all things whatsoever I have commanded you: and lo, I am with you always, even unto the end of the world. Amen.

Matthew 28: 16–20

That promise was made, not invented. It will mean a mind serener because He is standing by. It will mean a heart more loving to others because He loves us; and a heart more sensitive to the love of others through which He touches our lives. It will mean a will stronger to accept what has to be accepted, and to endure what has to be endured; it will mean that every experience of beauty, truth, goodness, love and joy has a new interpretation.

'Whatever stirs my heart and mind
Thy presence is, my Lord.'

I now affirm that presence and claim that promise.

LESLIE D. WEATHERHEAD

Granted is the Saviour's prayer, sent the gracious Comforter;
Promise of our parting Lord, Jesus now to heaven restored.

CHARLES WESLEY

Holy Spirit, hear us; help us whilst we sing,
Breathe into the music of the praise we bring.

Holy Spirit, prompt us when we kneel to pray,
Nearer come, and teach us what we ought to say.

Holy Spirit, help us daily by Thy might,
What is wrong to conquer, and to choose the right.

WILLIAM H. PARKER

100. Pentecost

And when the day of Pentecost was fully come, they were all with one accord in one place. And they were all filled with the Holy Ghost, and began to speak in other tongues, as the Spirit gave them utterance.

Acts 2: 1, 4

I was persuaded by a young Anglican priest to visit a young couple in his church. The happiness and assurance that radiated from them both was unmistakable. I asked, "What has happened to you people?".
"We went to a neighbourhood prayer meeting," explained Joan, her face lighting up even more at the memory, "but what impressed us most was this fellow named Bud... he was so happy—so sure of God, that he made us hungry to know what he had."
Her husband picked up the story. "Yes... So we asked him and he just said, 'Oh, I've been baptized in the Holy Ghost!' We didn't know what he was talking about. We didn't go to church very often, and we sure didn't know much about the Bible, but we were so attracted by what we saw that we said, 'We want it too'. He said, 'Let's pray about it'. So we did—and we DID!"
"Get baptized in the Holy Ghost you mean?" said I. "But what does that mean?" "Just like in the Bible," they said. That was a low blow! As a minister of the gospel, I was certainly supposed to know what was in the Bible. Yet as John and Joan talked, I realized that there were some important things I'd somehow missed...
(Cont. 101) D. J. BENNETT

Thy Holy Spirit, Lord, alone can turn our heart from sin,
His pow'r alone can sanctify and keep us pure within.

H. E. BLAIR

Holy Spirit, all divine, dwell within this heart of mine.

A. REED

101. The Gift of the Spirit

Then Peter said unto them, Repent, and be baptized everyone of you in the name of Jesus Christ for the remission of sins, and ye shall receive the gift of the Holy Ghost. *Acts 2: 38*

One of the ways I believe that the Spirit builds up through the use of tongues is by increasing our ability to praise God at all times. People come into this blessing in many different circumstances. Some as they are baptized in the Spirit, ome later.
Of all the gifts of the Spirit, Speaking in Tongues is the one which most people find hard to accept. We do not understand it, and it is a subject clouded with misconceptions. It is a gift of God and all God's gifts are good. (The word translated 'tongue' is the ordinary Greek word for language.) Certainly God would not ordain for His Church any thing that is harmful or unimportant. EDWARD SWINDALE

The reason John and Joan intrigued me so much, I mused, was that what I seemingly had lost, they had found—only more so. Maybe I'd better do a little research, I found that the early Christians were continually talking about the Holy Spirit. They were specific about the Holy Spirit—they didn't confuse Him with the Father, or with Jesus. I saw too, that the mysterious "speaking in tongues" kept cropping up. I found also that the early Church Fathers, my theology textbooks, and even the hymn books, now seemed to be full of references to the importance of the Holy Spirit. How did I miss it before? *(Cont. 102)* D. J. BENNETT

Mighty Spirit, dwell with me! I myself would mighty be,
Mighty so as to prevail where unaided man must fail.
Ever by a mighty hope, pressing on and bearing up.
THOMAS T. LYNCH

102. Gift of Tongues

If ye then, begin evil, know how to give good gifts unto your children, how much more shall your heavenly Father give the Holy Spirit to them that ask Him?

Luke 11: 13

Finally on a Saturday afternoon in November after three whole months of searching, I said to my enthusiastic friends: "I want what you've got! How did you get it?" John came across the room and laid his hands first on my head and then on my friend's. He began to pray, very quietly... I began to pray, as he told me, when a very strange thing happened. My tongue tripped... and I began to speak in a new language. Right away I recognised several things; first, it wasn't some kind of psychological trick... it was a real language... It had grammar and syntax: it had inflection and expression —and it was rather beautiful! I went on for about five minutes, then said to my friends: "Well! that must be what you mean by 'speaking in tongues'—but I don't feel anything!" They said joyfully: "Praise the Lord!"

D. J. BENNETT

The talented fisherfolk from the Church of the Redeemer at Houston (USA) did everything—testimonies, poetry, dancing, interpretations of new choruses, singing in the Spirit—all spiritual life was there. And they helped 1500 delegates, plus 180 day visitors, to forget personal tiredness and the hall's humidity and concentrate on the messages. RENEWAL 46

Lord... Thou hast promised that whoever asks shall receive... Now I am definitely asking you to fill me with the Holy Spirit.

103. Joy in Receiving

Then they that gladly received his (Peter's) word were baptized; and the same day there were added unto them about three thousand souls. *Acts 2: 41, 42*

'Three thousand souls'! As I write, I look at pictures of three thousand joyous faces packed together in Worcester Cathedral in the summer of 1973, at the Fountain Trust's Second Festival of Praise. And all round the world, from New Zealand to Canada, there gather happy congregations of Spirit-filled believers, praying and praising—young people and old. Are we Christians downhearted? Of course not. How could we be? Jesus is alive! The world is in God's hands!

According to the second chapter of Acts, two separate companies of people received the baptism, or gift, of the Spirit on the Day of Pentecost—a hundred and twenty at the beginning of the chapter, and the three thousand at the end. The three thousand do not seem to have experienced the same miraculous phenomena (the rushing mighty wind, the tongues of flame, or the speaking in other tongues). Yet they inherited the same promise and received the same gift (verses 33, 39).

JOHN R. W. STOTT

The Lord had promised the disciples 'Ye shall receive power, when the Holy Ghost is come upon you' Acts 2 describes a profound spiritual experience, the nature of which is not easily apprehended. But the results of the experience are quite evident. There came to the disciples a new sense of the Presence and the Power of God.

Source unknown

Oppressed with sin and woe, a burdened heart I bear;
In my Redeemer's Name, I give myself to Thee.

ANNE BRONTË

104. Healing Power

Then Peter said, Silver and gold have I none; but such as I have give I to thee: in the name of Jesus Christ of Nazareth, rise up and walk. And he took him by the right hand, and lifted him up: and immediately his feet and ankle bones received strength. And he leaping up stood, and walked, and entered with them into the temple, walking and leaping, and praising God. And all the people saw him walking and praising God.

Acts 3: 6–10

A man born lame, who had never known the joy of walking. At the 1973 Bible Convention at Frinton-on-Sea, Rev. W. Russell Shearer took this text for his Sunday evening sermon. How vividly he portrayed the man leaping with joy and praising God! He had been carried every day to the Gate to beg, and taken back to his poor home at night. Not often would he hear a kind word. And now he enters the Temple himself, not just watching others enter. He leaps and praises God.

This incident is one of a number which show the apostles continuing the healing work which Jesus did. Peter and John were so receptive to God's Spirit that powers of healing, hitherto unknown to them, were released through them.

International Bible Reading Association Daily Notes

I have had the wonderful experience of being healed—the healing of an eye. A Harley Street specialist could do nothing; but healing came through a friend with the gift of healing! When my own surgeon re-examined the eye later, the haemorrhage had completely cleared!

O Lord, we thank Thee for giving us each one a gift—the greatest is love for Thee and for Thy children, and this Thou truly hast given us.

105. Changed People

Then Peter said, Of a truth I perceive that God is no respecter of persons: but in every nation he that feareth him, and worketh righteousness, is accepted with him. The word, began from Galilee, after the baptism which John preached: how God anointed Jesus of Nazareth with the Holy Ghost and with power; who went about doing good, and healing all that were oppressed of the devil; for God was with him. While Peter yet spake these words, the Holy Ghost fell on all them which heard the word.

Acts 10: 34–38, 44 (selected)

What were the permanent results of the coming of the Spirit?

1. First, the transformation of the Christian fellowship; these very ordinary men were lifted out of themselves into a new fellowship in which they thought and experienced as one man.
2. The beginning of the Christian witness. Now they begin to proclaim the Resurrection from the housetops, though they do so at the risk of their lives.
3. The contagion of the new fellowship. Many of the crowd felt themselves irresistibly drawn towards and into this experience of which they had been the witnesses.

STEPHEN NEIL

Lord, I want the Spirit of power within,
Of love, and of an healthful mind:
Of power, to conquer inbred sin;
Of love, to Thee and all mankind;
Of health, that pain and death defies,
Most vigorous when the body dies.

CHARLES WESLEY

106. Courage through the Spirit

Now when they saw the boldness of Peter and John, and perceived that they were unlearned and ignorant men, they marvelled; and they took knowledge of them, that they had been with Jesus. And they commanded them not to speak at all nor teach in the name of Jesus. But Peter and John answered and said unto them, Whether it be right in the sight of God to hearken unto you more than unto God, judge ye. For we cannot but speak the things which we have seen and heard. And being let go, they went to their own company, and reported all that the chief priests and elders had said unto them... And when they had prayed, the place was shaken where they were assembled together; and they were all filled with the Holy Ghost, and they spake the word of God with boldness. *Acts 4: 13–20, 23, 31*

And this was Peter who was afraid of the maid of the High Priest—and of the second maid who recognized him. 'I know him not—neither do I understand what you are saying.' And he cursed and swore when others drew attention to his Galilean accent.

Now here he was with his friend, John—unlearned, both of them—speaking boldly and unafraid, speaking of Jesus and how through His power they had healed the man lame from his mother's womb. How? They had been baptized with the Holy Spirit—and that Baptism can be ours today.

Lord, thou art God, which hast made heaven, and earth, and the sea, and all that in them is... grant unto thy servants, that with all boldness they may speak thy word, by stretching forth thine hand to heal; and that signs and wonders may be done by the name of thy Holy child Jesus. *Acts 4: 24, 29–30*

107. Peter's shadow

And by the hands of the apostles were many signs and wonders wrought among the people; insomuch that they brought the sick into the streets, and laid them on beds and couches, that at the least the shadow of Peter might overshadow some of them. *Acts 5: 12, 15*

Many years ago those words first gripped me, at a Methodist Class Meeting when the Leader took for his subject Peter's shadow. He likened it to INFLUENCE, and as he talked I saw in my mind's eye the ever-increasing circles when a stone has been thrown into the water. People are influenced by us every day and that influence spreads to others. As I write, I inwardly see a small child at our garden-gate long ago. We had been away a month and how depressing to see the neglected bushes covered with greenfly! Then I looked round and saw the child. She was so full of joy and loveliness that my irritation just vanished. I returned to my task joyfully, and entered our home singing. You and I can either hurt or heal, give gloom or blessing. It is not what we say or what we do that has the greatest influence on others... it is just what we are that really matters. We all need the Holy Spirit radiating from us to reflect our dear Lord.

Fill Thou my life, O Lord my God, in every part with praise,
That my whole being may proclaim Thy being and Thy ways.
Fill every part of me with praise; let all my being speak
Of Thee and of Thy love, O Lord, poor though I be and weak.

HORATIUS BONAR

108. Stephen

And Stephen, full of faith and power, did great wonders and miracles among the people. Then they brought him to the council, and set up witnesses. Then said the high priest, Are these things so? And Stephen said, Men, brethren and fathers, hearken... When they heard these things, they.... gnashed on him with their teeth. But he, being full of the Holy Ghost, looked up stedfastly into heaven, and saw the glory of God. And they cast him out of the city, and stoned him. Stephen, calling upon God, and saying, Lord Jesus, receive my spirit, kneeled down, and cried with a loud voice, Lord, lay not this sin to their charge. And when he had said this, he fell asleep. *Acts 6: 8, 12; 7: 1, 54, 55, 59, 60*

What a lovely ending... *"He fell asleep"*. I have stood by the bed of the dying, but I have never seen *one* unhappy. They just seemed to fall asleep. My husband was ill for some years and a few weeks before he "slept" he called me to this bedside: 'Get a pencil and write this down quickly. I've just had a wonderful vision. Jesus came to me and said, 'Are you ready? I shall soon be coming for you!' Leslie Weatherhead used to say how foolish it would be for a baby in its mother's womb to be frightened of leaving the warmth and security of the 'nest', and worry about the outside world it was about to enter; likewise how foolish if we were to worry about leaving this world.

Lord, our God, we praise Thee for all that is past, and we will trust Thee for all that is to come, knowing that all will be well. Thou lovest these souls that we love with a love as far surpassing our own as the glory of noon surpasses the gleam of a candle. Therefore will we be still and trust in Thee. J. S. Hoyland

109. Dedication and something more

Then Philip went down to the city of Samaria, and preached Christ unto them. And the people with one accord gave heed unto those things which Philip spake, hearing and seeing the miracles which he did. For unclean spirits, crying with loud voices, came out of many that were possessed with them: many taken with palsies, and that were lame, were healed. And there was great joy in that city. *Acts 8: 5–8*

Now when the apostles which were at Jerusalem heard that Samaria had received the word of God, they sent unto them Peter and John: who, when they were come down, prayed for them, that they might receive the Holy Ghost... Then laid they their hands on them, and they received the Holy Ghost. *Acts 8: 14–17*

There was no doubt about the dedication to Jesus of the new converts in Samaria. But something was missing. In the last analysis this is what counts—not what we alone do, but what God, following on our commitment, does in and through us.

Internaiional Bible Reading Association Daily Notes

Give me, Lord, Thy Holy Spirit;
Sanctify me by Thy grace;
Guard me, guide me, help me onward
As I run my heavenward race.

R. J. LYON

O Jesus, Light of all below, Thou fount of living fire,
Surpassing all the joys we know, and all we can desire:
Thee may our tongues for ever bless, Thee may we love alone,
And ever in our lives express the image of Thine own.

BERNARD OF CLAIRVAUX

110. Saul of Tarsus

Saul desired of the high priest letters to the Damascus synagogues, that if he found any of this way, he might bring them bound unto Jerusalem. As he journeyed, suddenly there shined round him a light from heaven: he fell to the earth, and heard a voice saying, Saul, Saul, why persecutest thou me? Saul said, Who are thou, Lord? And the Lord said, I am Jesus whom thou persecutest. Saul arose from the earth; and when his eyes were opened, he saw no man, but they led him by the hand to Damascus...... There Ananias entered into the house; and putting his hands on him said, Brother Saul, the Lord, even Jesus that appeared unto thee in the way, hath sent me, that thou mightest receive thy sight, and be filled with the Holy Ghost.

Acts 8: 1–20 (selected)

What a marvellous true story. Read the Acts of the Apostles and see all that follows—how Saul's name was changed to Paul and how God mightily used him.

We Christians owe more than we can say to the changed life of Saul of Tarsus, who became so full of the Holy Spirit and power.

Sparked off by the martyrdom of Stephen, the opposition to the new faith now broke into direct and fierce persecution, and believers were scattered abroad. Jesus was not the kind of Messiah they wanted or were looking for. They wanted a forceful Leader like Joshua, not a suffering servant, as Isaiah prophesied.

International Bible Reading Association Daily Notes

Lord, we are filled with wonder at Thy ways and works. May we, too, have our eyes open and see Thy truth, and spread it to those around us.

111. The best gifts

Put love first; but there are other gifts of the Spirit at which you should aim also, and above all prophecy. When a man is using the language of ecstasy he is talking with God, not with men, for no man understands him; he is no doubt inspired, but he speaks mysteries. On the other hand, when a man prophesies, he is talking to men, and his words have power to build, they stimulate and they encourage. The language of ecstasy is good for the speaker himself, but it is prophecy that builds up a Christian community. I should be pleased for you all to use the tongues of ecstasy, but better pleased for you to prophesy. *1 Corinthians 14: 1–5, NEB*

It must mean something when there are so many miracles of love as prejudices and hatreds and fears are broken down. Not all problems are solved overnight, of course, but we accept and trust each other as brothers and sisters in Christ. Perhaps the most remarkable evidence of this was at the New Year conference in Co. Tyrone, when about a hundred Christians from different denominations and traditions came together. By the time they parted they were one in the Holy Spirit and rejoicing. *Renewal 45*

Come, Holy Ghost, our hearts inspire,
Let us Thine influence prove,
Source of the old prophetic fire,
Fountain of light and love.

Come, Holy Ghost, for moved by Thee
The prophets wrote and spoke,
Unlock the truth, Thyself the key,
Unseal the sacred Book.

CHARLES WESLEY

112. Praying in the Spirit (1)

If ye love me, keep my commandments. And I will pray the Father, and he shall give you another Comforter, that he may abide with you for ever; even the Spirit of truth; whom the world cannot receive, because it seeth him not, neither knoweth him: but ye know him; for he dwelleth with you, and shall be in you. *John 14: 15–17*

If every one that asks may find,
If still Thou dost on sinners fall,
Come as a mighty rushing wind;
Great grace be now upon us all.

CHARLES WESLEY

There came to me an experience that lifted my life to a new plane of understanding and of power. Twelve of us began to pray in a band, and the answer came by Pentecost. The key to all my life is in the experience. It awakened my mind as well as cleansed my heart. It gave me a new joy and a new power, a new love, and a new compasson. It gave me a new Bible and a new message. Above all else, it gave me a new understanding and a new intimacy in the communion and ministry of prayer; it taught me to pray in the Spirit. The work of the Holy Spirit is always in co-operation. He never works alone. He depends upon human co-operation for the mediation of His mind, the manifestation of His truth, and the effectual working of His will. The world is His, but the writing is with the hands of men.

SAMUEL CHADWICK

Spirit divine, attend our prayers,
O come, great Spirit, come!
Come as the dove, and spread Thy wings,
The wings of peaceful love.

ANDREW REED

113. Praying in the Spirit (2)

Likewise the Spirit also helpeth our infirmities: for we know not what we should pray for as we ought: but the Spirit itself maketh intercession for us with groanings that cannot be uttered. *Romans 8: 26*

God is here, and that to bless us
With the Spirit's quick'ning power!
See the cloud, already bending,
Waits to drop the grateful shower.

Those who pray in the Spirit must be in the Spirit, and if the Spirit of God is to make intercession for us He must dwell in us. The Spirit instructs all true prayer. There is no truer word than that "We know not what we should pray for as we ought". There is no realm in which we so soon come to the end of what we know as in that of prayer. The Holy Spirit knows the mind of Christ and the will of God, and He teaches us how to pray and what to pray for. The Spirit brings to expression the unutterable things of the soul. We are never really men of prayer in the best sense, until we are filled with the Holy Ghost.

SAMUEL CHADWICK

The Holy Spirit transforms our meagre resources. For commitment to Christ puts us into touch with His power... Don't limit yourself to the humanly possible. Remember that Christ's riches of wisdom and power are available for us...

Bible Reading Fellowship notes

Lord, send down Thy Holy Spirit to dwell in our hearts, we beseech Thee. May we be filled with Thy power and joy and enabled to do Thy will.

114. The Unity of the Spirit

In one Spirit we were all baptized into one body.
1 Corinthians 12: 13

They had all been baptized into one body. 'Body Christianity', and we mean by that a caring loving concern for our brothers in Christ, is the greatest need of the Church today. It is our deepest responsibility to work out and share in community what Christ has begun in us. This requires love, endurance, and great loving concern. *In the first number of "DUNAMIS"*

The Holy Spirit was there in power, gathering people together. There was ecumenical witness throughout the Conference. Who could forget the witness of four Protestant girls risking their lives to cross the invisible lines of hatred to pray with Catholic Christians? (Belfast and Dublin). The drive toward Christian unity in the charismatic movement, places the emphasis on spiritual ecumenism. At Nottingham (July 1973) it was evident that the movement was becoming mature. The Conference was more aware of the essential nature of the Church as the body of Christ and the people of God.
"Renewal 46"

God is here! O then believing,
Bring to Him our one desire,
That His love may now be kindled,
Till its flame each heart inspire.

J. L. BLACK

Lord, may we realize Thy truth—that we are all members of one body—if one suffers, all suffer; if one be honoured, all should rejoice; if one member truly loves, all members will be blessed.

115. Fruit of the Spirit

The fruit of the Spirit is love, joy, peace, longsuffering, gentleness, goodness, faith, meekness, temperance. If we live in the Spirit, let us also walk in the Spirit.

Galatians 5: 22, 23, 25

I have been thinking about these fruits of the Spirit: what would our life be like if we had none of them in the world? If no one had any love or joy or peace; if no one was longsuffering, and no one gentle or good; if we had no faith in anything or anyone, and if folk were overbearing and never meek! And horrors! if no one had self control. That is one of the disasters brought about by drink. If only drinkers realized that the intoxicant lessens the power of the brain so that they can control neither themselves nor their cars! What a world it would be to live in! I stayed once at an orchard in Tasmania, at the time of the grading and packing. Not one bad apple did I see; the trees had been attended to daily the whole year round, not just occasionally. If we would have a good harvest, our trees need daily care, food, drink, pruning. So the fruits of the Spirit beginning to grow in us need daily food, the daily elimination of all that is harmful, the sunshine of God's love and the showers of blessing. God loves us, but He seeks our love in return and the fruits of His Spirit must be tended.

O Jesus Christ, grow Thou in me,
And all things else recede.
My heart be daily nearer Thee,
From sin be daily freed.

JOHANN C. LAVATER

116. Spirit of Love

Hereby know we that we dwell in him, and he in us, because he hath given us of his Spirit. And we have seen and do testify that the Father sent the Son to be the Saviour of the world. Whosoever shall confess that Jesus is the Son of God, God dwelleth in him, and he in God. And we have known and believed the love that God hath to us. God is love; and he that dwelleth in love dwelleth in God, and God in him. Herein is our love made perfect, that we may have boldness in the day of judgment; because as he is, so are we in this world. There is no fear in love; but perfect love casteth out fear.

1 John 4: 13–18

Love is the vital force upholding all creation and the initiative of loving is always with God.

Bible Reading Fellowship notes

Love Divine, all loves excelling,
  Joy of heaven, to earth come down:
Fix in us Thy humble dwelling,
  All Thy faithful mercies crown:
Jesu, Thou art all compassion,
  Pure unbounded love Thou art;
Visit us with Thy salvation,
  Enter every trembling heart.

CHARLES WESLEY

O Lord, who hast taught us that all our doings without charity are nothing worth, send forth Thy holy Spirit and pour into our hearts that most excellent gift of charity.

Collect of Quinquagesima, Book of Common Prayer

117. The Family of God

For as many as are led by the Spirit of God, they are the sons of God, For ye have not received the spirit of bondage again to fear; but ye have received the Spirit of adoption, whereby we cry, Abba, Father. The Spirit itself beareth witness with our spirit, that we are the children of God: and if children, then heirs; heirs of God, and joint-heirs with Christ; if so be that we suffer with him, that we may be also glorified together.

Romans 8: 14–17

When I read those lovely words of Paul my thoughts go back to our little Methodist chapel on the Yorkshire Pennines, and I see our dear Minister, now called to higher service, telling us in his talk to the children how the word "Abba" was like saying "Daddy"—a pet name for "father". He made God seem so near and dear to us.

At the hearthside all the children are equal. No true parent has a favourite child... All are equal at home... And God holds us all in equal love; black and white; red or brown; male and female. One family we dwell in Him.

W. E. SANGSTER

Lord, you have chosen us,
You have made us sons
With all who call you Father.
Help us to throw off the slave mentality,
Give us the spirit of adventure,
The confidence of sons and heirs,
So that we live
In the power of your Spirit
Within us.

J. S. HOYLAND

118. Power over Temptation

But God is faithful, who will not suffer you to be tempted above that ye are able; but will with the temptation make also a way to escape, that ye may be able to bear it.

1 Corinthians 10: 13

I find tremendous help in those words. We are all tempted, but we are promised strength, and a way to escape. Read Luke 4: 1—13 The first verse declares that Jesus was full of the Holy Ghost: this was why in the wilderness He was able to say sternly to Satan, "Get thee hence!" and "for a season" Satan did depart. (This "for a season" suggests that Satan tried again at other times!) Read Hebrews 4: 14–16. In His Father's strength Christ overcame all temptation. So if we have Christ in our hearts, and His Holy Spirit, all will be well with us And with every temptation we resist, I find, we are stronger to meet the next!

Here in the maddening maze of things,
  When tossed by storm and flood,
To one fixed ground my spirit clings;
  I know that God is good!

And if my heart and flesh are weak
  To bear an untried pain,
The bruised reed He will not break,
  But strengthen and sustain.

J. G. Whittier

In Thy strength, O God, and with the Holy Spirit in our hearts, we will *go forward. No Satan can ever resist Thee! Evil can never conquer Good.*

119. Temples of the Holy Spirit

Know ye not that ye are the temple of God, and that the Spirit of God dwelleth in you? If any man defile the temple of God, him shall God destroy; for the temple of God is holy, which temple ye are.

1 Corinthians 3: 16, 17

What? Know ye not that your body is the temple of the Holy Ghost which is in you, which ye have of God, and ye are not your own? For ye are bought with a price: therefore glorify God in your body, and in your spirit, which are God's. *1 Corinthians 6: 19, 20*

Many of us live on a level lower than our Spirit-Baptism makes possible because we do not remain filled with the Holy Spirit. We need to repent and return to God. The fullness of the Spirit is intended to be not a static but a developing experience.

JOHN R. W. STOTT

O come, O Holy Spirit, come!
Come as holy fire and burn in us,
Come as holy wind and cleanse us,
Come as holy light and lead us,
Come as holy truth and teach us,
Come as holy forgiveness and free us,
Come as holy love and enfold us,
Come as holy power and enable us,
Come as holy life and dwell in us.
Consecrate us, until we are wholly Thine
For Thy using, through Jesus Christ our Lord.

ADAPTED BY CHARLES FRANCIS WHISTON
FROM AN ANCIENT PRAYER

O Breath of God, breathe on us now, and move within us while we pray. The spring of our new life art Thou, the very light of our new day. ALFRED H. VINE

120. The Trinity

Go ye therefore, and teach all nations, baptizing them in the name of the Father, and of the Son, and of the Holy Ghost. *Matthew 28: 19*

Holy, holy, holy, Lord God Almighty!
Early in the morning our song shall rise to Thee;
Holy, holy, holy, merciful and mighty.
God in Three Persons, blessèd Trinity.
REGINALD HEBER

From the earliest years of the Church the threefold blessing was in use. The grace of the Lord Jesus Christ, the love of God, the fellowship of the Holy Spirit.... these men were devout Jews and never departed from the central conviction of Judaism. God is one. But One in Three, and Three in One. Creator; Redeemer; Sanctifier. The Father in majesty; the Son in suffering; the Spirit in striving. And it was from the Church's experience that this doctrine arose. It wasn't fashioned... to make a simple thing difficult for ordinary people. 'This is how we met God', said the Apostles. W. E. SANGSTER

Teach us to know the Father, Son, and Thee, of both, to be but One;
That through the ages all along this, this may be our endless song:
All praise to Thy eternal merit, O Father, Son, and Holy Spirit! ANON

O Trinity! O Unity! Be present as we worship Thee;
And with the songs that Angels sing unite the hymns of praise we bring. J. D. CHAMBERS

The grace of the Lord Jesus Christ, and the love of God, and the fellowship of the Holy Spirit, be with us all.